"Dr. Parent teaches simple and clear lessons that can be applied to your game right away. He gives you a new and better approach than other theories of sports psychology."

—Charles Howell III, PGA TOUR Rookie of the Year 2001

"Deeply insightful but easy to understand, this book will help golfers of all levels improve their putting and the rest of their game."

—Michael Hunt, Lead Master Instructor, Jim McLean Golf Schools

"There is a lot more to being a great golfer than mechanics. Dr. Joe's writing and teaching go right to the heart of what you need to know to master the mental game."

—Dave Licalsi, Senior Instructor for Dave Pelz Golf

"I relied on Dr. Parent's mental principles to keep my cool and win the men's senior club championship in a playoff."

—Steve Lewis, The Olympic Club, San Francisco

"I was stunned. 76 . . . best-ever score at a course without windmills. The round had been easy and stress-free. As I signed my scorecard, the sky seemed much bluer than it was supposed to be . . ."

—Connell Barrett, *Golf* Magazine
Editor-at-Large, after lessons with Dr. Parent

HOW TO
MAKE
EVERY
PUTT

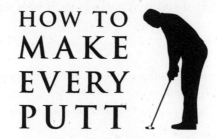

ALSO BY DR. JOSEPH PARENT

ZEN GOLF: Mastering the Mental Game
ZEN PUTTING: Mastering the Mental Game on the Greens
GOLF: The Art of the Mental Game

HOW TO MAKE EVERY PUTT

THE SECRET TO WINNING
GOLF'S GAME WITHIN THE GAME

DR. JOSEPH PARENT

GOTHAM BOOKS

GOTHAM BOOKS
Published by the Penguin Group
Penguin Group (USA) Inc., 375 Hudson Street, New York, New York 10014, USA

USA | Canada | UK | Ireland | Australia | New Zealand | India | South Africa | China
Penguin Books Ltd, Registered Offices: 80 Strand, London WC2R 0RL, England
For more information about the Penguin Group visit penguin.com.

LIBRARY OF CONGRESS CATALOGING-IN-PUBLICATION DATA
has been applied for.

ISBN 978-1-592-40822-1

Printed in the United States of America
10 9 8 7 6 5 4 3 2 1

Set in Adobe Garamond Pro
Designed by Spring Hoteling

While the author has made every effort to provide accurate telephone numbers, Inter-
net addresses, and other contact information at the time of publication, neither the
publisher nor the author assumes any responsibility for errors or for changes that occur
after publication. Further, the publisher does not have any control over and does not
assume any responsibility for author or third-party websites or their content.

Neither the publisher nor the author is engaged in rendering professional advice or
services to the individual reader. Physical activity may result in injury if done improp-
erly or if not suitable for your particular physical condition. Accordingly, before beginning any exercise regimen or breathing techniques, and/or if you feel pain or discomfort
while exercising, it is recommended that you consult your healthcare professional. Neither the author nor the publisher shall be liable or responsible for any loss or damage
allegedly arising from any information or suggestion in this book.

To my life teachers

Chögyam Trungpa
and Ösel Tendzin,

who showed me the way
to see clearly, to feel deeply, and
to act with caring, conviction,
and confidence

CONTENTS

SECTION III: YOU'D BETTER WATCH YOUR SPEED

SECTION IV: LET'S GET THE BALL ROLLING

SECTION V: THE BEST PUTTING ROUTINE EVER

SECTION VI: THAT ONE LOOKS A LITTLE TRICKY

SECTION VII: GETTING BETTER ALL THE TIME

BONUS CHAPTER: ONE FOR THE YIPPER

ACKNOWLEDGMENTS

There are many people to whom I am grateful for their contribution to the development of this book. Whatever capability I have of teaching others that may be expressed in this work I learned from my teachers, the Venerable Chögyam Trungpa, Rinpoche and the Vajra Regent Ösel Tendzin (Thomas Rich Jr.).

I will always be grateful to my dear friend and fellow coach, Ed Hanczaryk, one of Canada's top 50 teaching professionals. It was his encouragement when I began coaching that inspired my career path.

To Jack and Barbara Nicklaus, much appreciation—to Jack for the inspiration of his unsurpassed mental game, and to Barbara for her unsurpassed graciousness and kindness.

There can't be a teacher without students or a coach without players. To the many golfers who were willing to think outside the box and entrusted their games to our work together, I am deeply grateful. Much appreciation to Vijay Singh and Cristie Kerr, who recognized and applied what *Zen Golf* and my personal coaching had to offer in their climbs to No. 1 in the world, as well as many other touring professionals, including David Toms, Juli Inkster, Hunter Mahan, Christina Kim, Tim Petrovic, Julieta Granada, Carlos Franco, Brian Gay, Jerry Kelly,

Tommy Armour III, Brian Wilson, Willie Wood, Luke List, Beth Allen, Clare Queen, Alejandro Quiroz, Jason Schultz, David Berganio, Jon Fiedler, Shane Bertsch, and all the other tour players with whom I've worked and made friendships over the years.

Thanks to my colleagues, other coaches that have shared their insights and inspirations, including Bryan Lebedevitch, Fran Pirozzolo, David Leadbetter, Jim Flick, Jim McLean, Eddie Merrins, Rob Akins, Stan Utley, Michael Hunt, Trillium Sellers, Mike Meehan, Glen Albaugh, Ray Carrasco, Tom Barber, Tom Szwedzinski, Katherine Roberts, Conan Elliott, Jason Carbone, and many others. Special thanks to Nick Middleton, who makes the superlative Zen putting products I use for coaching and playing.

To Michael Murphy, author of *Golf in the Kingdom*, to Steve Cohen, founder of the Shivas Irons Society, and to all its members, appreciation for their genuine love of the beauty and mystery of golf, and for inviting me into their clan.

To Mark Greenslit, Jeff Johnson and all the staff at the Ojai Valley Inn & Spa in Ojai, California, and to Kirk Reese, Jim Schaeffer, Justin Davidson, and all the staff and members of The Los Angeles Country Club, thank you for welcoming me to teach at your marvelous golf courses and learning facilities.

Thanks to the many dear friends who have supported and encouraged my work over the years: Patrick Sweeney, Edward Sampson, Jeff Herrick, Glen Kakol, Lyle Weinstein, Kathryn Butterfield, Avilda Moses, Ladye Eugenia Stewart, Arlene Dorius, Brad Pennington, Steve Lewis, Randy Sunday, Irv and Leah Mermelstein, Ken and Betty Potalivo, and many more. Special thanks to my dear friend Diane for her loving support that means so much.

Thanks to those who have been willing to offer to help increase awareness of my teaching through their celebrity, including Ray Romano, Kevin James, Malcolm McDowell, George Lopez,

Robby Krieger, Michael Bolton, Kenny G, Michael O'Keefe, Anthony Anderson, Robert Hays, and Patrick Warburton, to name a few.

Many thanks to my publisher, Bill Shinker, and my editor, Jessica Sindler, of Gotham Books, for their vision, guidance, and support. Great appreciation to my literary agent, Angela Rinaldi. She is also a gifted editor and friend who has provided great encouragement in the completion of all of my books. Angela, you're the best.

I am very grateful to fellow author and golf partner Ken Zeiger, for generously putting his time and energy into going over the manuscript with me again and again to make it the best it could be.

Thanks to Erik Lang for shooting and editing the video segments of drills and demonstrations that accompany selected chapters in this book. A golf student and filmmaker, he has been kind enough to feature my work in his documentary *Golf: The Hole Story*.

To those in the golf media: Peter Kessler, David Marr Jr., Rich Lerner, Jaime Diaz, Susanne Kemper, Fatiha Betscher, Connell Barrett, Bill Pennington, Josh Sens, Guy Yocom, Al Barkow, Bob Buttitta, Michael Arkush, Rex Kuramoto, John Paul Newport, and others, many thanks for making my work known to a wider audience.

Last but not least, deep gratitude to my whole family for their encouragement in all my work. Mom and Dad, my sister, Nancy, and my brother, Jack, have all been tremendously supportive and encouraging of my teaching and writing.

INTRODUCTION

Putting is often spoken of as golf's game within the game. The putting stroke is the least complex of all the ways there are to swing a golf club, yet no other shot in golf elicits as great a range of idiosyncratic, one-of-a-kind techniques as you see on the greens. Putting is as much an art as it is a technical skill.

While few can hit a drive with the ability of a top professional, almost anyone has the capability to stroke a putt as well as the best. It requires no special strength, speed, size, or dexterity. That's why the mental game is a greater factor in determining success or failure in putting than it is in any other type of golf shot. A poor drive can be remedied by a great approach shot; a poor approach can be remedied by a great chip shot. There is no remedy for a missed four-foot putt. And the closer you get to the hole, the more pressure there is.

The opening of the classic television show *Wide World of Sports* promised drama in "the thrill of victory and the agony of defeat." In golf, the green is where that ultimate drama unfolds, where the biggest thrills and greatest agonies reside. A pressure-packed putt holds the potential for either the most frustrating or the most rewarding feeling you can have at the end of a hole, a round, or a tournament.

The techniques I'll show you in *How to Make Every Putt: The Secret to Winning Golf's Game Within the Game* include updated and revised versions of those that I presented in *Zen Putting: Mastering the Mental Game on the Greens*. I'll also give you new lessons and exercises that I've developed since the publication of *Zen Putting*, featuring my step-by-step formula for the latest and greatest putting routine ever. All of these methods have evolved from my continuing work with both top golf professionals and amateurs of all levels, from beginners to state champions.

How to Make Every Putt is a collection of lessons that let you find your own way to confidence in putting. The chapters are organized by theme, starting with the key elements of my unique approach that allows you to "make every putt," and ending with a bonus chapter for emergencies—the yips. However, each chapter is also its own independent topic, so you can move from one chapter to another in whatever order satisfies your personal needs and interests. You'll find exercises, drills, and routines that you can use while warming up, on the practice green, and even at home on the carpet.

When reading this book and applying the techniques, please remember that this is a collection of lessons for golfers of all levels. The techniques are intended to offer you a range of possibilities to explore, all for the purpose of helping you improve your putting. What works best for one person may not be all that helpful for another; it's up to you to decide what to incorporate into your personal putting routine.

The opening section of *How to Make Every Putt* explains the critical differences in my unique definitions of "making" a putt versus "holing" a putt. I'll help you understand these and other parts of the proper mind-set for developing true confidence on the greens. You'll learn a simple but highly effective technique for changing unhelpful habit-patterns into useful, positive, and repeatable actions.

The central sections of *How to Make Every Putt* reveal the secrets to reading greens, judging speed, and making a proper putting stroke. I'll explain the key elements of a great putting routine, and teach you some outside-the-box techniques that will help you deal with especially challenging situations on and around the greens.

The last section of *How to Make Every Putt* focuses on working toward continuous improvement in putting. You'll learn the PAR approach to getting out of your own way and getting better as you play. Finally, if you suffer from that unfortunate condition known as the yips, I've included a bonus "emergency" chapter that provides the remedy. So take heart—there is hope.

At the beginning of each section and in many chapters you'll find quotes from or anecdotes about many golfing greats, including several each from Jack Nicklaus, Bobby Jones, and Bobby Locke. Knowing how great putters go about their craft is something I find inspiring.

I hope you'll enjoy trying the various techniques and practicing the exercises in *How to Make Every Putt*. You'll find a new level of confidence on the greens, and that in turn will lead to a better attitude about the rest of your game. When you truly feel that you can make every putt, you'll be well on your way to the satisfaction of more consistency, less frustration, and lower scores.

HOW TO USE THIS BOOK

Multimedia Functions

How to Make Every Putt includes video demonstrations of many of the lessons and exercises featured throughout the book. For those reading the hardcover edition, you can use your mobile device to scan the provided QR Square bar code at the end of selected chapters.

The link will take you to the video for that chapter within the online video library of drills and demos for this book. Even without a smartphone or tablet, you can still view all these videos. Go to www.HowToMakeEveryPutt.com, the web address for the online index of chapters and videos from which you can access the clips you'd like to watch. For those of you reading the eBook edition, just click on the live Watch the Video link at the end of selected chapters.

HOW TO MAKE EVERY PUTT

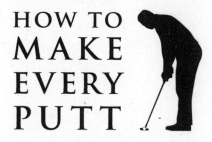

SECTION I

HOW TO MAKE EVERY PUTT

Jack Nicklaus once commented that he had never missed a crucial putt on the last hole of a tournament. When someone in the audience reminded him of a specific situation in which he had missed such a putt, Nicklaus replied, "I didn't miss that putt. I made the putt—the ball missed the hole."

THE SECRET TO MAKING EVERY PUTT

Confidence is the feeling that you can make every putt. When golfers are asked for their definition of "making" a putt, the nearly unanimous response is, "The ball going in the hole." I'd like to change that. The ball going in the hole should be the definition of *holing* a putt. The definition of *making* a putt should be, "The ball starting out on the line you chose, at the speed you wanted, with what you felt was a good stroke." If you rolled the ball the way you intended, you *made* your putt.

The secret to *making* every putt is to focus only on successfully executing your routine and stroke, not letting your concern about the outcome of the putt interfere with how well you're doing that. Take care of your process and let the results take care of themselves.

Because golf greens are imperfect surfaces, even seemingly perfect putts don't always go in the hole. So your experience of success in putting should be determined by the way the ball started rolling rather than the way it ended up. If your confidence is based only on how often the ball falls in the hole, you are in trouble. It is far better to focus on getting the ball started the way you want to. That is something you can control.

The three keys to *making* a putt are line, speed, and stroke. You want to get it started on the line you determined from your reading of the green for slope. You want it to be rolling at the speed you intended based on your feel for the distance. And you want your stroke to produce a true roll from the sweet spot of the putter.

After the ball has traveled just a foot or two, you'll know how well you executed the three keys. If you did so successfully, then you *made* your putt, whether or not it went in the hole. You know you won't hole every putt, but you can *make* every putt. And the better job you do at *making* a putt, the better chance you'll have of holing it.

Exercise: Keep track of how many putts you *make* during your next round of golf according to this new definition. Did you get the ball started with the line, speed, and stroke you intended? To emphasize execution, a pro I coached gave himself one point for *making*—but just half a point for holing—each putt. Track your success this way and you'll have confidence when you get to the green.

ALREADY IN THE HOLE

I never stroked a putt that I hadn't already made in my mind.
—Jack Nicklaus

Many golfers have experienced the feeling of intuitively know-ing that a putt, particularly one that has some length and break to it, is going to go in. It's a moment when you feel like you know the future. It doesn't matter how you stroke the putt—there is no way that it is *not* going in the hole. It's a sense of certainty: not a hunch, not something you figured out, not something you have to try hard to make happen.

Everything seems simple. You don't have to figure out the way the putt will break; you just see it. You feel calm and fo-cused at the same time. Your rhythm is natural and unforced. You are fully present without distraction.

This calm certainty is never the result of effort. It's not something you can manufacture—you're not *trying* to concen-trate. Instead, it comes from your intuition, not from an ana-lytical, self-conscious mind. You can't crank it up, but you can *invite* this feeling. By laying the groundwork and creating the right atmosphere, you allow it to arise more easily.

This experience can happen even in the midst of fierce competition. It is a combination of ease and intensity, a little glimpse of being in the Zone. It's a great feeling.

The best way to encourage being both calm and focused involves visualization. And the best way to visualize is to "see" the ball as already having rolled into the hole. When you see in your mind's eye that the ball is already in the hole, there is no need to *try* to get it into the hole. There are no thoughts about the ball missing the hole. You're free to let your body execute what you want to accomplish without trying too hard or being overly careful.

The more you develop trust in yourself, have unconditional confidence in your ability, and let your instincts take over, the more often that feeling of certainty will come to you.

Exercise: Use this "Connect the Dots" drill as a way of getting better at visualizing putts.

- Imagine the line you expect a breaking putt to take, then set ball markers at points along the line, every foot or two.

- Connect the dots in your mind to get a clear image of the line you think the putt will take, and then focus on getting the ball started on that line.

- Watch how the ball actually rolls out, then adjust the ball markers to create a more accurate line.

- Continue practicing this way until the putt rolls right along the line made by the markers and into the hole.

Soon you will be able to see the line of each putt without placing the markers. You'll learn to read putts more accurately, visualize the line more clearly, and have more fun watching your ball rolling along that curving line you pictured, right into the hole.

What Did You Expect?

Your mind chooses to pay attention to what you expect to see, to what matches the way you think about your world and yourself. If you are angry at someone, you'll notice all the things they do that irritate you or that you think they're doing wrong. But you won't notice the nice or competent things they do.

If you're expecting failure on the green, you'll see the many ways your putt can miss—long, short, low side, or high side—instead of seeing an ideal line and speed for it to go in the hole.

When your experience matches your expectations, it gives you confirmation that the way you see things is accurate. Getting that kind of confirmation is such a high priority that you will ignore or dismiss great amounts of evidence to the contrary. You will exaggerate the importance of even one instance that matches your view of how things are. If you think of yourself as a poor putter, it will take many rounds of good putting to begin to feel like you are actually good at putting. But hit just one or two badly missed putts and you'll feel like you are just as bad as you thought.

Expectations are based on memories, and emotions give memories extra weight, a higher priority in how easy they are to recall. Missing a three-footer to lose a playoff in a tournament will have a much longer-lasting effect than a three-footer missed on the very same hole in the first round. Whatever you have the biggest emotional investment in is what you will remember the most. Negative memories accumulate each time you get upset about missing a putt.

Golfers remember all the poor putts they've hit, and start seeing their putter as "that thing I miss putts with." Holding that putter, they expect to see a poor putt. They start thinking about how to not hit a bad putt, rather than how to hit a good one. That's a recipe for a hesitant, uptight stroke.

You can affect the way you selectively remember things by intentionally directing the energy of emotion in a positive way. Focus your energy on appreciating the positive aspects of your experience, and be more calm and matter-of-fact about the negative aspects. If you get energized about your good putts, you'll remember more of them. The more good putts you remember, the more confident you'll be about the next putt.

Exercise: Practice the proper reactions after each putt.

- When you hit a good putt, whether it went in or not, be positive about how it felt. You're reinforcing the feeling that you've done a good job executing your process, which imprints a positive memory.

- If the putt wasn't struck well, don't beat yourself up about it. Get into the habit of reacting less emotionally to a poor putt. Look instead for what interfered with your ability to make a good putt. Before leaving the green, replace the negative experience of the poor putting stroke with a practice stroke that feels better.

- If the ball misses the hole, be more reflective and detached from the experience, giving it less emotional power. If you hole the putt, direct your energy to how well you executed your process with positive emotion, strengthening your memory of success.

Get Real to Get Confidence

Most golfers have unrealistic expectations when it comes to putting. Television contributes to the problem by fostering the illusion that professional golfers hole a great percentage of their putts from long distances. It seems that way because only the players in contention—the ones who are playing their best and holing lots of putts—are on camera. On top of that, when the broadcast does switch to someone who is not on the leaderboard, it's usually to show the golfer holing an amazingly long and difficult putt that was recorded earlier.

When a tour player has a putt of about sixteen feet that's relatively straight, it's common for television commentators to say, "That's a very *makeable* putt." Well, every putt is makeable, and every putt is missable. The problem is that they are misleading their audience into thinking that if it's struck properly, there's a very good chance that the putt will go in. Actually, there's a better chance that it won't. The fact is that on average, the pros only hole a sixteen-foot putt once in every five attempts. The "makeable" comment creates a false expectation of the realistic chance of holing such putts.

The PGA TOUR collects statistics of the percentage of putts holed from various distances. The numbers haven't changed much over the last decade:

8 feet = 50%; 10 feet = 40%; 12 feet = 30%; 16 feet = 20%; 24 feet = 10%

Aren't we being too hard on ourselves for missing an eight-foot putt when the best golfers in the world miss them half the time? And is it realistic to compare ourselves to pros in the first place?

The Challenge: When you have unrealistically high expectations about putts you think you should hole, missing them causes you to become self-critical. With unnecessary pressure on yourself, you start missing easier putts, and then lose confidence in your putting altogether. Heading down this unfortunate path is a result of mistaken thinking and is a self-perpetuating cycle of disappointment.

The Solution: There's no point in getting frustrated at missing a so-called *makeable* putt when the best players in the world miss them far more often than they hole them. Instead, think of every putt as makeable only in terms of the quality of execution: line, speed, and roll. That's all you can control. As for the results, recognize the realistic chances of holing that putt, and don't be too hard on yourself if it doesn't fall.

Get realistic about putting percentages. Lower your standards for holing putts to reduce your frustration, and raise your standards for your quality of execution to increase the effort you put into your process. You'll replace frustration with confidence, make the most of your abilities, and get the best results.

For long, challenging putts, it's helpful to pre-accept an area around the hole as a successful result. Start the putt with the intention of holing it, but be satisfied that getting it close enough to avoid a three-putt is a good outcome.

Exercise: Keep track of the length of each of your putts as you play. Review your percentages and see if there are particular putts you struggle with more than others. Then spend some time practicing putts of those lengths, and you'll see your overall putting results improve.

When it comes to putting, everyone has habits—some good, some bad. The ideal putting routine is a series of good habits. Improving your putting is a matter of changing one or more habits in your routine or stroke. You may need to stop doing something unhelpful, like decelerating at impact. You may want to develop a helpful habit, like keeping a light, consistent grip pressure throughout the stroke. What's the best way to make those changes?

Habits are actions that feel like second nature—they're things you do without having to think about them. They're also deeply ingrained, so it can take some time and effort to change them. When you change a habit and start doing things differently, it usually feels unnatural and awkward. If a student complains that a change doesn't feel right because it's uncomfortable, I ask, "How well was comfortable working for you?" The challenge is having the willpower and discipline to stick with a new technique through the initial awkwardness until it becomes second nature.

The essential components in changing a habit are determination, awareness, and freedom from negative judgment.

You need determination to keep up your discipline, because new habits feel uncomfortable. You need a strong desire to make any change.

You need awareness to recognize any habitual behavior that interferes with your performance. Notice how often that habit occurs, and you'll catch yourself sooner and sooner. Eventually, the impulse driving the habit will fade.

You need to be free from negative judgment, because whenever you direct emotional energy toward a habit, you strengthen it. Don't berate yourself when an unhelpful habit recurs, but do congratulate yourself when you do something positive.

To apply nonjudgmental awareness and disciplined intention to a habit you want to stop falling into, chart the number of times that habit occurs in each round. Without negative judgment, the strength of the habit will diminish, and you'll do it less frequently. To encourage something you want to happen more often, reinforce the habit by giving yourself positive feedback every time you do it.

You know in the back of your mind that you'll be accountable after each putt for the quality of your process. For that reason, you'll be more likely to catch yourself before you start an unhelpful habitual behavior, and you'll be more likely to engage in a helpful habit that you want to develop.

Exercise: On your scorecard, write a word or phrase that describes the habit you want to change. As you play, mark down a letter that represents the habit each time you notice it occurring. For example, if you have a habit of leaving putts short, write "Short Putts" on your scorecard and mark a letter *S* every time you leave a putt short.

If you're trying to develop the habit of holding your finish after each putt, write "Hold Finish" on your card and give yourself positive feedback by making a checkmark each time you do it well. It will feel good to see those checkmarks adding up.

It's also important to remember that when you're working to change a habit, your results will be inconsistent at first. It is essential to trust your basic abilities and have patience with the process.

Over the course of several rounds, as your habits change and your routine improves, you'll see improvement in your scores as well.

PUTT WITHOUT CARING

Hit the putt as well as you can, and do not allow worry over the outcome to spoil the stroke.

—Bobby Jones

Some tour pros say that they putt their best when they don't care if they miss. It's hard to believe that they wouldn't care when they're playing for a small fortune at every tournament. But to "care" can either mean "to have an interest in," or "to worry about." What those pros actually mean when they say they don't care is that they're not worrying. It's natural to care about whether or not you'll hole your putt. The point is not to worry about it.

On the other hand, we can get careless. Some golfers try to trick themselves into not worrying. Pretending not to care, they just walk up and carelessly hit the putt. That's a mistaken approach that usually produces a poor result.

Don't kid yourself. Of course you care—if you didn't, you wouldn't be playing golf. But you can care without worrying, so that you'll be able to focus and commit to your process without anxiety about the outcome.

The right approach is to be carefree—the middle way between careful and careless. Carefree means zeroing in on the way you want to get the putt started while staying free of worry about the outcome. You'll putt your best when you commit to your judgment of the line and speed of the putt, then set up and stroke the putt without fear or hesitation.

Trust your routine, focus only on how you want to get the putt started, and there's a much better chance that your stroke will be smooth and steady. If you're free from worry about whether or not the putt will go in, you'll find that it goes in more often.

Exercise: During your next round, take a moment after each putt to think about how you felt just before you stroked it. On your scorecard or yardage book, mark a letter *M* for each time you were fully focused on *making* your putt: line, speed, and roll at the start. Mark a *W* for each time you were *worried* about how the putt would turn out. As you mark down more M's and fewer W's, your putting will be marked by more confidence and less worry.

Section II

Those Are the Breaks

I examine the line of the putt, concentrating particularly around the hole, where the ball completes its run. Having carefully assessed the hills and hollows along the path, I marry the picture I get of ground contour to the picture I already have of the speed of the putt, until I form a clear mind's-eye view of the ball running across the green and into the hole.

—Bobby Locke

THE SECRET TO READING GREENS

Putting is a guessing game. You can't be certain exactly how the slope or the grass surface will affect the ball until after your putt is done. All you can do is make your best guess of the combination of line and speed, put your best stroke on it, and see what happens. To have the feeling we talked about earlier, that the ball is "already in the hole," you need confidence in your ability to read the green.

When reading a putt, the order to follow in judging line and speed isn't set in stone. You may first get a sense of how fast the ball needs to roll to reach the hole, then an idea of how far to the right or left you need to start it. That view may change your sense of speed. For example, you may decide that the putt needs a bit more speed to get far enough up the slope before it starts breaking toward the hole.

How you prefer to see the ball go in the hole also affects the way you read putts. A putt that slows as it nears the hole will break more than a putt that is holding its speed all the way to the cup. Do you prefer playing less break and more speed, seeing the ball zip into the cup like a homesick mole? Or would you rather play more break and less speed, seeing the ball slow to a crawl before it just topples in over the edge? You'll be more consistent at both reading greens and stroking putts if you settle on a consistent way of playing the combination of speed and line for a breaking putt.

Exercise: Explore different speeds and lines to discover the most comfortable combination for you. Practice reading breaking putts from different distances. For each putt, try different lines on which to start the putt until you find the combination of break and speed that lets you hole the putt most consistently and leaves you a reasonable second putt when you miss.

Through this exercise you'll find the amount of break you're most comfortable playing for different distances and for the steepness of the slope. Being more comfortable makes it easier to commit to your read, which allows you to make a more confident stroke. And nothing is more important in putting than confidence.

THE LAY OF THE LAND

I start reading a putt when I'm still fifty yards from the green.
—Jack Nicklaus

Always read your putts from the biggest view to the smallest. Look at the lay of the land around the course, the high and low points around the green, the contours around the line between the ball and the hole, and finally the last few feet of the putt. Let all that information percolate in your mind until an image arises that is your best guess of how the ball will make its journey toward the hole.

Learn from the nearby landscape. Water always seeks the lowest level, so putts tend to break toward greenside lakes or ponds. In general, look to see how water would drain from the area of the green near the hole—the ball will tend to go in that direction.

A subtle aspect of the lay of the land concerns the area of the green nearest a greenside bunker. Greens are usually designed so that water will not drain off the green and into a bunker, so the edge of the green near a bunker will be slightly elevated. Also, sand is continually being thrown from the bunker onto the fringe of the green during play. Over time that raises the surface near the bunker slightly. Take both of those factors into account when the line of your putt passes near a greenside bunker—the ball will tend to turn away from it.

The Challenge: The effects from distant landscape features aren't as obvious as those around the green. There will be a subtle slope toward the ocean, even if it's miles away. Putts that look flat will break away from distant mountains. In some cases the lay of the land can create an optical illusion, making it look like putts are breaking uphill.

The Solution: If you know about aspects of the distant landscape that subtly affect the slope of the greens, learn that direction and keep it in mind when you're looking at the lay of the land around the green. A special note for "away games": When you arrive at a course you haven't played before, ask someone in the pro shop about the lay of the land. Is there a direction toward which the greens on the course generally break?

Exercise: Here's a technique to help improve your green-reading skills. It uses your imagination to change your perception. Set a ball about twenty feet from a hole on a relatively flat portion of green. While still looking in the direction of the hole, imagine as vividly as you can that there is a mountain just to the left of the green, and a lake just to the right of the green. You'll see the green as having a very slight tilt away from the mountain and toward the lake. Then imagine the reverse: a mountain on the right and a lake on the left. Notice how your perception changes from one imaginary landscape to another.

It may be a very subtle effect, but awareness of the lay of the land when you read the green can make the difference between a putt that just misses and one that rolls right into the center of the cup.

It is always a good practice to borrow generously from any slope and attempt to cause the ball to pass a tiny bit above the hole. There is always a chance it will fall into the upper side, and it is certain that it will stop not far away. But once a putt begins to roll below the hole, every inch it travels carries it further from that precious cup.

—Bobby Jones

For steep sidehill putts, take Bobby Jones's advice and play the maximum amount of break that allows the ball to reach the hole on the high side. If the ball doesn't go in, you will likely have a short, low-stress second putt. If you play less break and the putt misses on the low side, the same-speed putt will roll out farther from the hole.

Putts that have a lot of break require that you only concern yourself with the first half of the putt. You have to roll the ball up the hill just far enough to get it into position to turn down the slope. In the second half of the putt, gravity will carry it down to the hole.

Start by going behind the hole. Look back toward the ball and see the line that it would be most likely to take to fall in the high side. From there, follow the line backward until you come to the apex, or high point, of the break. That's the point at which the ball stops heading uphill along its line and starts to turn and roll downhill toward the hole.

To judge the speed for the full length of the putt, make your best guess as to how big a stroke you need to send the ball to the apex of your intended line, and add on just a little for it to go the rest of the way. It's all downhill from there.

On the practice green, experiment with breaking putts. Gradually increase the amount of break you play on a particular putt, up to the highest apex that still allows the ball to reach the hole. Keep in mind that it's important to minimize stress during a round. As Bobby Jones pointed out, putts that miss below the cup roll farther past it than those that go by on the high side. And it's less stressful to have a second putt of six inches than six feet.

Exercise: An ordinary scorecard can be used as a helpful training aid. Lay the card so that it covers half the hole, with the edge of the card going across the center of the hole on a line that points straight at the ball. The open half of the hole should be on the high side for your putt. Looking at the hole with the low side covered makes it easier to see the line into the high side. Roll a series of putts, starting with a small amount of break. Gradually adjust the line of each putt for more and more break until you find the ideal line. You'll see how much easier it is to hole breaking putts when you take the high road.

Rivers and Fountains

Once a putt starts to break, you generally expect it to keep breaking. It can be very frustrating to watch your ball turning and turning as it rolls downhill toward the hole, but then see it straighten out just before it gets there and miss on the high side. Another frustrating putt is one that climbs straight uphill, but then breaks to one side and misses the hole just before reaching it.

The patterns of these frustrating misses resemble the natural flow of rivers and fountains. Recognizing them will help you make better reads and hole more putts. Downhill putts will take a curving line to start and then straighten at the end, like curving creeks that eventually join a river and flow straight downstream. Uphill putts will take a straight line to start and then curve sharply at the end, like the straight streams of a fountain that turn outward as they near their peak.

Downhill Like a River: Go below the hole on downhill breaking putts and try to find the *fall line*—the line on which a ball would roll straight down the slope of the green. Picture your putt breaking toward the hole until it gets to the fall line, and then see it straighten out after that.

Since it's a downhill putt, you can roll it to the point where it meets the fall line, after which gravity will help it feed to the hole. In that way, it's like a creek joining a river, curving until the water enters into the main current and is carried along from there.

Practice by finding the fall line on a sloping area of the putting green. Then try a variety of putts at different distances from the hole and different angles to the fall line, seeing how far above the hole your putt can meet the fall line and still feed all the way down to the hole.

Uphill Like a Fountain: Go just above the hole, and find a spot a foot or two past it on the through line of your putt. The *through line* is the line through the center of the hole on which the ball would roll if the hole weren't there. When you set up for your putt, look at that spot as your target instead of the hole. If the putt keeps up its speed on the through line toward that spot, the hole will be in the way and the ball will fall in. In that way, it's like a fountain, the stream of water shooting straight up for most of its journey, turning only as gravity slows it and makes it head back toward its source.

You can practice this type of putt using a recently replaced hole-plug on the practice green, one that clearly shows the outline of where the hole used to be. Watch the path that the ball takes across the old hole, and you'll soon know how to visualize the fountain effect.

Using the patterns of rivers and fountains to read your putts will help you picture their lines more accurately, so you'll get to see more of them flow into the cup.

SPLIT THE DIFFERENCE

When you read a putt from behind the ball and then go behind the hole to read it from that direction, the break will occasionally look very different. In some cases, it will actually look like it breaks in the opposite direction. Which read should you believe?

The Challenge: Obviously, two different reads of the same putt can't both be correct. There is an optical illusion at work here, based on what you perceive when you read the line of your putt from two different directions. It's often accentuated when the putt is steeply uphill or downhill. Looking from opposite directions gives you conflicting impressions about the green's surface. When you judge the slope of the green based on these different looks, the results can be quite contradictory.

The Solution: There are theories about always trusting one direction for reading versus the other: from behind the hole versus behind the ball, or looking uphill versus looking downhill. In my experience, no one way is correct all the time. What I recommend is to split the difference.

If it looks like the putt will break a lot when viewed from behind the ball, but very little when viewed from behind the hole, or vice versa, split the difference and read the break to be halfway between the two. For example, if at first a putt looks like it will break about six inches, but then appears to be straight when you read it from the other direction, play for three inches of break.

Sometimes it looks as if a putt will break in two different directions. In this case, you could be facing a *double-breaker*—the first part of the putt breaks one way and then the rest of it breaks the other way. Or it may be that the putt is straight, with no break at all. In either case, the best strategy is to split the difference: Set up with the putterface aimed at the middle of the hole and make a good stroke for the speed you intend.

The most important thing to do is to remove whatever doubt you have about the line and make a decisive choice about how much break you're going to play before you start your routine. Whatever line you choose, commit to it fully and *make* your putt. After that, all you can do is root for it to go in, and learn from it if it doesn't.

Take It with a Grain

The grain of the greens, the direction in which grass leans as it grows, affects the speed and break of putts. You can identify the direction of the grain by the sheen of the surface: When it looks dark and dull you're looking into the grain, when it's light and shiny you're looking with the grain. Another way to identify the direction of the grain is to look at the edge of the hole. The side that looks more ragged is the side toward which the grain runs, because you're seeing the cut roots of the grass leaning away from the hole. The opposite side of the hole has a smoother looking edge because you're seeing the tops of the grass blades that are leaning toward the hole.

In general, grass tends to lean toward the setting sun and toward nearby ponds or creeks, so you can look for the grain to go that way. Bermuda grass greens tend to be grainier than bent grass, but the roll of the ball on any green that isn't very fast and smooth will be influenced to some extent by grain.

The Challenge: The difficulty in dealing with grain is that you have to stroke level putts as though they're uphill when putting against the grain, or downhill when you're putting with the grain. You have to play straight putts to break when putting across the grain. That means you need to override the instinct to act according to your perception.

The Solution: When putting against the grain, give the ball enough speed for it to pop firmly into the back of the cup, or make your target distance a spot on the green a foot or two past the hole. When putting with the grain, give the ball just enough speed for it to trickle over the front edge of the cup.

Putting across the grain is trickier. The slower the putt is rolling, the more the grain will influence it. Commit to one of two choices: Play for the effect of the grain, or stroke a firmer putt to reduce the grain's influence. It's hard to play for break on what looks like a flat putt, but you can use visualization to make this easier. Imagine a mound on the side of the line of your putt from which the grain is growing, or picture a strong wind blowing across the surface in the same direction as the grain. This will create a different perception of the line of the putt, and you'll be better able to trust your read and commit to the stroke.

Exercise: There is no substitute for direct practical experience of the influence of grain on the speed and break of a putt. Find a grainy practice green and experiment with the solutions given above. As you become more accustomed to seeing how your putts react to grain, the ability to read those putts will become more ingrained in your mind.

READ WITH YOUR FEET

It's news to many golfers that they can use their feet as well as their eyes to read a putt. Champion golfer Bobby Locke, known for his great putting skills, mastered this technique decades ago. One instance of this was described by Al Barkow, an honored golf writer, who was watching Locke read a lengthy putt at the Open Championship in 1972 at Muirfield: "As he walked all the way to the cup, [he] kept pressing his feet in a kind of never-leave-the-ground tap dance to get the speed of the green as he peered down looking for grain." After walking back the same way, "he rapped the ball to within two inches of the cup. Beautiful!"

The Challenge: As presented in the chapter "The Lay of the Land," some factors that influence the slope of the green can create optical illusions. When there is uncertainty about your read, it's hard to commit to your line and speed.

The Solution: Get more information from your sense of feel by reading with your feet. Walk between the ball and hole to the side of—not directly on—your initial read of the line of your putt. Some golfers find it helpful to walk first toward the hole on one side of the line of the putt and then back toward the ball on the other side. With your awareness focused on your feet and your balance, feel how much or how little the slope of the ground tilts you one way or the other, and how much you sense that you're walking uphill, downhill, or on level ground.

Merge what your feet are telling you with what your eyes are seeing. Sometimes your eyes can play tricks on you, so if in doubt, you may want to put your faith in your feet.

Exercise: To place as much of your awareness as you can into your feet and your sense of balance, you may find it helpful to work with your breathing. You can use the "Center of Gravity" exercise I introduced in *Zen Golf: Mastering the Mental Game*. Take a full breath in and, as you slowly breathe out, feel the weight of your upper body moving down, as if your center of gravity is settling at the level of your belly. With the next breath, feel your center of gravity moving even lower and settling in your hips and legs. With one more breath, feel your weight pressing down into your feet, and your feet pressing against the ground.

Try this two or three times, with breaks in between so that you don't hyperventilate. When it feels familiar, practice moving your awareness down into your feet in just one breath.

When you're on the course and want to read the green with your feet, take one full breath to move your awareness into your feet. You'll be able to feel your line as well as see it, and you'll have more confidence when you stroke your putt.

GO TO SCHOOL

Most golfers know that it's time to "go to school" when a fellow competitor is putting before them on a similar line. This means carefully watching the way the other player's putt rolls in order to get more information on how their own putt might break. However, few golfers realize that they can also learn from watching a putt that starts on a line perpendicular to their own. Seeing the way such a putt reacts in the area immediately around the hole can provide valuable knowledge.

Watch a putt that is perpendicular to yours as it nears the hole. If it breaks toward your ball, you know that your putt will be going uphill as it approaches the hole. If the putt breaks away from your ball, your putt will be going downhill at the hole.

If the perpendicular putt slows as it approaches the hole, your putt will break in the direction from which the other putt came. If the perpendicular putt holds its speed as it goes by the hole, your putt will break in the direction that the other putt was heading.

Perpendicular putts give you the little bit of extra information that can mean holing a putt you would otherwise have missed, so they are well worth watching.

Exercise: Use the following "Sidehill Circle Drill" to improve your green reading skills. On the practice green, set eight balls evenly spaced in a circle around a hole that is on a moderate slope, with each ball about six feet from the hole. Work your way around in a circle, rolling each putt in sequence. Notice how the break changes subtly from putt to putt. As explained in the earlier chapter "Rivers and Fountains," the putts up or down the fall line will be straight. With each putt around the circle moving farther from that line, the amount of break will be greater. Practice this drill going around the circle in one direction, then the other. Train your green-reading skills by setting a goal to practice the "Sidehill Circle Drill" until you can hole eight in a row. Before long, you'll be able to go to school on any putt from any direction.

Section III

You'd Better Watch Your Speed

Loren Roberts, a PGA TOUR and Champions Tour winner, was such a good putter that his nickname was "The Boss of the Moss." When asked what he felt were the three most important things in putting, he answered without hesitation, "Speed, speed, and speed."

THE SECRET TO SPEED

The secret to speed is hand-eye coordination. In sports that involve throwing a ball, you look at your target while you're throwing. What you see gives you a feel for the distance you want the ball to travel. Your brain sends messages to your muscles based on the picture it gets from your eyes, and your muscles react by doing their best to propel the ball the distance you want it to go. The better your hand-eye coordination, the better your chances of an accurate throw.

The Challenge: When making a putting stroke, instead of looking at the target, you're looking down at the ball near your feet. How can you use your hand-eye coordination to help you get a better feel for the speed of a putt?

The Solution: The secret is maintaining an image in your mind of the distance you want your ball to roll once you look away from the target and toward the ball. This includes a sense of how steeply uphill or downhill the putt is, and how fast or slow the surface is. That will provide the "eye" part of your hand-eye coordination: the visual sense of the speed of the putt that will give you the feel for how big a stroke you want to make.

To have the best feel for the speed of a putt, read the green for the slope, grain, and the pace of the putting surface. Include the way you want the ball to enter the cup: trickling over the front edge, pouring into the middle, or popping into the back. Once you've got your line and you set up to the ball, follow this sequence:

- Take a good long look at the distance you want the ball to roll.

- Look down toward the ball and bring to mind a picture of the target distance.

- Stroke the putt with that picture in mind.

This routine is ideal for tuning in to a feel for speed through your hand-eye coordination.

Exercise: This "Guessing Game for Feel" creates a feedback cycle between your visual perception and your feel for speed. Place a few balls on a level area of a practice green about twenty feet from the fringe of the green. Set up to one of the balls, and take a long look at the distance between the ball and the fringe. Then look down at the ball and make what you think is the right size swing to roll the ball just to the edge. As soon as the ball is on its way, *without looking*, guess out loud where you feel that the putt will end up, saying, "Short," "Long," or "About right." Only after you've guessed should you look to see how it actually turned out. Getting this kind of visual feedback is the most effective way to learn how much bigger or smaller to make your next swing. Repeat until you're rolling putt after putt "about right." To enhance your feel, do this exercise with uphill and downhill putts as well. The hand-eye coordination you develop will help you to trust your feel and make confident putting strokes.

How Fast Is This Green?

In addition to slope and grain, another factor that influences your feel for the speed of the greens is how smooth and slick they look to you. But looks can be deceiving. If the greens are actually faster or slower than you judge them to be, you'll need to adjust your sense of the speed accordingly.

The Challenge: If the greens are slower than they look, you may find yourself saying again and again, "That putt sure looked faster than it turned out to be." You could spend half your round leaving putts short before convincing yourself that you need to roll them with a bit more speed. What can you do to make that adjustment sooner?

The Solution: You need to override what you think you see with what you know to be. Here's how to get a feel for how much the speed of the greens matches or differs from what your eyes are telling you. As you approach the practice green, first guess how fast or slow the green looks to you in comparison to other greens you've played on. Then toss two or three balls from the fringe onto an open area of the green.

As the balls roll out, you'll have an expectation of when they're likely to come to a stop. If they stop sooner than you thought they would, you'll know the green is slower than it looks. If they keep on rolling farther than you expected, you'll know the green is faster than it looks.

It's more helpful to toss them from your hand than to roll them with your putter. The direct hand-eye feedback will give you the most precise feel of the difference between how fast the green looks and how fast it actually is.

Apply whatever you learned when you get out on the course. Before each putt, remind yourself that the speed of the green is faster or slower than it looks, and adjust the stroke you make accordingly.

Exercise: For an enhanced sense of the speed of the green, squat down near the fringe and roll a few balls onto the green, one at a time. You can get a worm's-eye view of how each ball rolls, which will show you how bumpy or smooth the green is and how the ball reacts if the green is grainy. That will give you the information you need to have a good feel for the speed of the greens from the start of your round.

Sometimes the greens on the course are faster or slower (usually faster) than the practice green. If you find that to be the case, make an adjustment based on the difference between your expectations and the results you get from your first couple of putts.

Swing Bigger, Not Harder

The speed of a putt comes from the transfer of energy from the putterhead to the ball. Naturally, you'd think that to roll a putt farther, you'd need to swing at the ball harder. Not necessarily.

Hitting hard at a putt reduces your sense of feel for distance because you have to tighten your grip to move the putterhead faster. It also makes the roll less consistent because the sharp hitting action at the ball produces skidding and wobbling. The urge to hit at the ball interferes with your rhythm and tempo. Making a smooth and rhythmic stroke means more consistency in how the ball starts on its way, resulting in more consistency in the speed at which it rolls.

You'll find it much simpler and more effective to maintain the same tempo, grip pressure, and swing path for every putt. For different distances, the only adjustment you need to make is to let the putterhead move back and through on a longer or shorter arc.

The Challenge: If you've been using a small stroke with a hard hit on long putts, changing to a stroke with a much bigger arc can be a little scary. That's because it's unfamiliar, and you may fear that your distance control will get worse with a bigger swing. Or you may tend to tighten up on the way down, afraid that you'll hit the putt too far. That fear will also cause you to decelerate the putterhead as it nears the ball.

The Solution: Resolve to maintain your tempo and grip pressure for every putt. Practice making different size swings to get used to how far the ball rolls for each. Just let the putterhead fall along the arc and through the ball, without giving it any extra juice at impact. You'll be surprised at how big a swing you can make and still not hit the ball too far when you keep your grip pressure soft and consistent. It will soon be more comfortable to swing bigger, not harder.

Exercise: The following "Leapfrog Drill" develops the connection between speed and the size of your stroke. Place two tees in the practice green about six paces apart as the start and finish points for the game. From a few paces back, roll a putt just past the first tee. Then roll additional putts, trying to make each one go just barely past the previous putt. The objective here is to make the same basic putting stroke while increasing the size of the swing by a little bit for each successive putt.

Try to fit in as many balls as you can before you go past the second tee. You get a point for each putt that passes the previous ball, and lose a point for every putt that doesn't get past. The game ends when a putt rolls beyond the second tee. Use different starting distances, and keep trying to improve your best score. It's also a good idea to play the "Leapfrog Drill" as a contest with a friend, which will introduce some competitive pressure to simulate real golf experience.

POUR, TRICKLE, AND POP

Whenever you read a putt with some break in it, you're not just reading for line. You're also reading for speed. How much a putt breaks depends on how fast it's rolling. The faster the ball is traveling, the less effect gravity will have on it and therefore the less it will break. How do you choose whether to stroke a putt gently and play the maximum break, or to stroke it firmly and play the minimum break?

Deciding on the way you want the ball to go into the hole—pour into the middle, trickle into the front, or pop into the back—means a trade-off between the pros and the cons.

When the ball is rolling at a slow enough speed to just trickle in when it gets to the hole, it's likely to fall in if it hits the side edge of the cup. That makes the effective size of the hole larger. However, the slower the putt, the greater the risk that any imperfections in the green will send the ball off line.

When the ball is rolling fast enough to pop into the back of the cup, it will probably hold its line even if it hits a bump in the putting surface. However, if it hits the side edge of the cup, it's likely to lip out. That makes the effective size of the hole smaller.

When the ball is rolling at a speed that allows it to pour into the hole—not too fast and not too slow—it will tend to hold its line better than the putt that just trickles in. There's also less chance that the putt will lip out, which often happens when you try to pop one into the back of the cup.

The Challenge: When you're under pressure, you might decide that you need to give a putt some extra speed on an uphill slope, or make an extra gentle stroke on a downhill slope. Thinking that way can do more harm than good and cause you to adjust your stroke as the putterhead reaches the ball.

The Solution: Make any adjustments in the size of your stroke *before* you address the ball, not while you're swinging the putter. Use visualization to fine-tune your feel for the speed you want.

For putts that are uphill or into the grain, or on particularly slow greens, visualize the ball popping firmly into the back of the cup. This will help you make a bigger but smoother stroke without having to give the ball a little extra hit to make sure it reaches the hole.

For putts that are downhill or with the grain, or on particularly fast greens, imagine the ball just trickling over the edge of the cup. This will help to prevent you from tensing up and decelerating the putterhead out of fear that the ball will roll too far.

Decide how you want the ball to go into the hole, pre-accept the pros and cons that go with your choice, and commit to rolling the ball at that speed.

Exercise: Set three balls about four feet from a hole. Practice rolling them so that they go into the hole at three different speeds: pour, trickle, and pop. When you feel you've done a good job at that distance, repeat the exercise for six-foot putts. Keep increasing the length of the putts. This will give you a good feel for how big a swing to make for the speed you need.

GIVE IT A CHANCE

You may have heard a television commentator, after watching a putt roll six feet past the hole, say, "I guess he felt like he had to give that one a chance." If the putt went that far, did he really *give it a chance*?

A common misconception regarding that expression is that you should hit the putt with a lot of extra speed so that you guarantee it won't stop short of the hole. Unfortunately, when the ball is traveling at a speed that would take it more than two feet past the hole, your chances of holing the putt are worse, not better. If it catches the edge it will probably spin out. You may even get a "power lip-out"—the ball picks up speed as it goes around the rim of the hole and, like a slingshot, shoots down the slope of the green even farther than if it had missed the hole completely.

Studies have shown that a putt has the best chance of going in when the ball is traveling at a speed that would carry it about a foot-and-a-half past the hole if it misses.

Also keep in mind that the likelihood of missing the comebacker increases as the ball goes farther and farther from the hole. Tournaments have been lost on the final green by golfers who thought they had to *give it a chance* to make a birdie—and ended up three-putting for a bogey.

The Challenge: You decrease rather than increase your chance of holing a putt when you give it too much speed. It's a problem if you try to take a bigger stroke than you normally would for a putt of the length you are facing. When you make an extra big swing, you might panic on the way down to the ball, hold back, and end up leaving the putt short. When you take a normal swing but are afraid that the ball won't reach the hole, you might hit extra hard at impact and send it speeding by. In either case, you're thinking too much about results and getting in your own way.

The Solution: Any thoughts of giving a putt something extra or worrying about leaving it short are added baggage. It's a much better idea to stay with your routine as you would for any other putt. If you want some assurance that you won't leave it short, the only adjustment you should make is in how you picture the ball entering the hole. For a downhill putt, visualize the ball pouring into the cup rather than trickling in. For a level or uphill putt, picture the ball popping firmly into the back of the cup rather than pouring in. Then go through your regular routine and do your best to *make* the putt you intend. After that, root for it to go in just the way you pictured it.

Exercise: Practice giving your putts the best chance of going in by training yourself to putt at a speed that carries the ball a foot or two past the hole. Give yourself a point for every putt that either rolls into the hole or stops less than two feet past it. Take away a point for any putt that is short of the hole or more than two feet past it. Keep track of your scores for putts of various lengths. Also practice the "Guessing Game for Feel" (see page 35) and "Leapfrog Drill" (see page 39) exercises to improve your feel for speed. When you get on the course and want to be sure that you *give the putt a chance*, you'll know what that really means and how to really do it.

I Can't Believe I Left Another One Short

A very common reason that players leave putts short is that they are too careful. They tighten up and make a tense, restricted stroke. When you're putting *for something*—a birdie, the match, your personal best score—the added pressure can cause interference with your ability to make the free, smooth putting stroke you intended.

If you have doubts about the speed or line you've chosen, you will be hesitant because you're fearful of making a mistake. Hesitation in the mind becomes deceleration in the stroke—you hold back as you near impact. Deceleration can also happen if your grip tightens because of the intensity of your hope and fear about the putt. It's as if you're holding on for dear life.

The way your vision works can also cause you to leave putts short. When you focus too tightly on the hole, the distance appears shorter than it really is. You then play for that incorrect distance, and the putt comes up short. Another common tendency is not to see anything beyond the hole. It's as if the hole is the end of the world for that moment, and you hold back to keep the putt from going so fast that it goes over the end of the world.

Leaving a putt short may also be a subtle way to protect your ego. You know you'll feel badly if the ball goes by the hole and doesn't go in. If it goes by the hole, you can't deny the fact that you missed. However, if you leave the putt short, if it never reaches the hole, you can always say, "I would have made it if I'd just hit it a little more firmly." In a subtle mental manipulation to protect your ego, you tell yourself that you didn't really miss the hole—you just left it short.

The Challenge: Being overly concerned about the outcome of a putt makes you try to guide the ball toward the hole instead of simply swinging the putter down the line. Fear of going past the hole makes you decelerate as you near impact. In either case, the likely result will be a putt that ends up woefully short.

The Solution: Strengthen your commitment to the speed and line you've chosen and trust your ability to stroke the putt well. Recognize that thoughts of hope or fear about the outcome of the putt are making you uptight. Replace them with the picture of the line you've chosen, the feel you want for the stroke, and the rhythm of your routine. Stick with your process and you'll be less likely to let concern for results interfere with your stroke. If you are free from worry about how the putt will turn out, you won't decelerate as you strike the ball.

Exercise: Expand your vision to see the full space of the green. Seeing the space on the green beyond the hole allows you to make a free and fearless stroke. Stick a tee in the green two feet past the hole. Get the feel of a stroke that will roll the putt to that tee on a line through the hole. Focus on maintaining the speed of the putterhead through impact, without deceleration. Send the ball on its way without fear and you won't have to say, "I can't believe I left another one short!"

SECTION IV

LET'S GET THE BALL ROLLING

Once I've started the putter in motion, it's as if it's swinging itself.

—Ben Crenshaw

The best way to make a stroke that repeats consistently is to have as few moving parts as possible. You don't really need to get your body into it to roll a putt, unless it's very long or steeply uphill. Also, the less you can involve the twitchy small muscles of your hands and forearms, the better. The ideal body setup therefore includes a stable base of legs and torso with a steady head and spine angle. The ideal position of the putter in relation to the arms creates a capital *Y* shape, with the puttershaft vertical and each arm extending down to it from shoulders that parallel the intended line of the putt.

Swing the putterhead *through* the ball, not *at* the ball. Feel as if you're *sending* the ball toward your target. After impact, the putterhead should chase the ball down the line.

At the end of the stroke, hold the finish for a couple of seconds, rather than letting the putterhead fall to the side or pulling it back toward the starting position. Keep your head steady until the putt is well on its way. Then, without raising your torso, just turn your head to the side to watch the putt roll out, hopefully into the hole.

The Challenge: Pushing or pulling a putt off line can be caused by either the path on which the putterhead is traveling during the stroke or the direction in which the putterface is pointing at impact. When the shoulders move left or right during the stroke, the path of the putterhead is redirected. When the hands are active during the stroke because of excessive tension, they often turn the putterface at an angle to the swing path, imparting a glancing blow at impact.

The Solution: When making the stroke, use the forward shoulder as a kind of tracking guide. With the forward shoulder moving straight up and down, there will be no swinging across the line, neither inside-out nor outside-in. The putterhead will move consistently along the swing path.

Maintain the capital *Y* shape of your arms and the putter-shaft so that the hands aren't involved. When the hands aren't involved in exerting force or directing the putter during the stroke, they won't twist the putterface, and you'll send the ball directly where the putterface is pointing.

Exercise: In practice and when warming up for a round of golf, always start by *putting to nowhere*. Bobby Jones recommended that "there is no finer practice for developing a reliable putting stroke than putting without a hole—just dropping a number of balls on a green or carpet and stroking them back and forth. Relieved of the need for finding and holding the line, the entire attention can be given to the club and the manner of swinging it."

Roll some putts toward an area of the green where there is no hole. Make average-size swings, find your most comfortable tempo, and keep your grip soft and your head and body steady. Then roll a few shorter and longer putts, maintaining the same feel and tempo for all of them. Keep putting to nowhere until you feel that your stroke is rhythmic and consistent, with the ball coming off the sweet spot of the putterface time after time.

Don't Hit It—Send It

> The putting stroke is not intended to be an act of hitting at the ball, but rather a feeling of sweeping it along the green. It's as if you're swinging a little broom with soft bristles instead of striking a nail with a hammer.
>
> —Bobby Jones

Putting is like a relay race. In a relay race, all you can do is run as fast as you can, and then make as good a handoff of the baton as possible. After that, the outcome is beyond your control. In putting, swinging the putter as well as you can is like running your leg of the race. Transferring energy through the putterhead to the ball with the best swing path and impact position possible is like making that good handoff of the baton. After that, all you can do is watch the ball go on its way and root for it.

In the relay race of putting, the way in which you transfer energy to the ball is important. Ideally, you want to feel that you're *sending* the ball along your intended line as part of a smooth stroke, rather than *hitting at* the ball with the putterhead.

During a golf tournament broadcast, a commentator was complimenting PGA Champion David Toms on his putting technique, saying, "There's one of the few players whose putting stroke really looks like his practice stroke, like he's swinging the putter without a ball there. The putter just swings and the ball happens to be in the way."

The Challenge: If you are hitting at the ball, the ball is your target. If the ball is your target, there is a tendency to stop all the action at the ball. That's what it means to be "ball-bound." You are so concerned about impact with the ball that you lose track of speed and direction.

The Solution: Think of *sending* the ball along the line rather than hitting at the ball. If you're sending the ball along the line, the target is at the end of the putt. If the target is in the distance rather than at the ball, the swinging movement of the stroke sweeps through the ball and continues down the line. The intention of sending the ball frees you from being ball-bound and helps you stay connected with the image of the ball rolling into the hole. You'll make a better stroke with a better feel for the speed of the putt, and have a better chance of winning the relay race of putting.

Exercise: Go through a routine of alternating putting strokes with and without a ball. Make a practice stroke, feeling the transition at the end of the backswing and holding the finish at the end of the follow-through. Then set up to a ball and do your best to swing the putter the same way through the ball, sending it along the line. Repeat these alternating strokes until you can consistently reproduce the feel of your practice stroke in your actual stroke through the ball. Then vary your swing size for putts of different lengths. Connect to your target in the distance while maintaining the same flow and tempo through the ball that you had in your practice stroke.

In the regular swing, many golfers use the overlap grip, in which the entire front hand (the hand closer to the target) is on the shaft, with the back hand directly below it and the little finger of the back hand overlapping the index and middle fingers of the front hand. The most common putting grip, the reverse overlap grip, has the entire back hand on the shaft, with the front hand directly above it and the index finger of the front hand overlapping the ring and little fingers of the back hand.

The Challenge: The back hand is usually your dominant hand, the one you use for more tasks than the other. When the back hand exerts more force than the front hand during the stroke, it can cause the front wrist to bend, which can flip or twist the putterhead at impact. This tendency is further exaggerated when nervousness, excitement, or other emotions arise as you prepare to putt.

Many golfers also have a tendency to open their shoulders farther than they should (meaning the back shoulder is closer to the ball than the front shoulder) when the back hand is below the front hand. A line across the shoulders in such a setup will point well away from the intended line of the putt, requiring compensations in body motion to keep the putterhead swinging on a straight path.

The Solution: If you use the back-hand-low grip and tend to set up with your shoulders open to the line, try switching to the forward-hand-low grip. You may find that it helps square your shoulders so that they parallel the intended line of the putt.

Putting with the forward hand low also reverses the leverage that the hands have on the puttershaft, which can help prevent the dominant hand from making the forward wrist bend. You may find this grip to be even more effective if your hands are just barely touching or even very slightly separated on the shaft.

Over the years, a wide variety of alternative methods to grip the putter—all designed to reduce the influence of the dominant hand in the execution of a smoothly flowing putting stroke—have evolved. The colorful names of these are usually descriptions of the way in which the back hand is placed on the puttershaft, including "the claw," "the paintbrush," "the saw," and "the pencil."

Keep in mind that a new way of gripping your putter can feel uncomfortable at first. As we discussed in "How to Make Changes," it takes patience and discipline to make a change. However, seeing putt after putt roll into the hole will help you get comfortable pretty quickly.

To prevent deceleration, I recommend a grip called "the point," which can also help you maintain a straight swing path. This grip used to be called "the whiskey finger." Golfers who were shaky in the morning from too much drink the night before believed that this grip steadied their stroke. Extend the index finger of your back hand straight down the back of the shaft, so that the putter is like an extension of your finger. As you swing, you should feel as though your finger is pushing the putterhead through the ball. To maintain a straight swing path, your finger keeps the putter pointing down the line of the putt after impact. To prevent decelerating at the ball, imagine that your finger and the putterhead are moving through a candle flame—if you slow down, you'll get burned!

Not Too Tight, Not Too Loose

Sam Snead said that you should hold a golf club with the same pressure you'd use if you were holding a small bird: softly enough not to hurt it, and firmly enough not to let it fly away.

When you hold your putter softly, it's easy to feel the weight of the putterhead at the end of the shaft. That translates into better feel for speed. By maintaining that same amount of pressure throughout the stroke, it's less likely that you'll guide or hit at the putt with your hands. It's best to hold the putter as softly as you can without feeling like it's out of control.

I make a point of using the word *soft* rather than *loose* to describe the way you hold the putter. The word "loose" brings to mind a lack of control. However, you can hold the putter softly and still feel that it's under control. It's ideal to feel that your wrists are firm enough to keep the angle between the shaft and your arms constant, while your hands are soft enough to maintain feel.

I also prefer to say that you *hold* the putter rather than *grip* it. To *grip* brings to mind a sense of grasping tightly, which is the opposite of what you want to do.

The Challenge: It's easy to maintain the same pressure throughout the swing when you're making a practice stroke because there's no ball to hit! It's the hitting action that makes you tighten up just before impact. If you pay attention, you'll notice that when you hit at the ball, you've tightened your hold on the putter to do so. When you suddenly tighten your hold before impact, you alter the path of the putterhead as it moves through that point in the swing, which sends the ball off line.

The Solution: Hold the putter as softly as you can while still feeling that you can control the path of the putterhead as you swing it. On a 1-10 scale of soft versus firm, it generally works best for it to be below 5. Then pay attention to your grip pressure as you stroke a putt. Work at maintaining the same pressure all the way through, especially around the point of impact with the ball.

Jack Nicklaus imagined that the shaft of his putter was like the thin stem of a crystal wineglass. If his grip tightened at all during the stroke, the crystal stem would snap. That's an image that gives you a good feel for holding the putter softly and consistently throughout your stroke.

Exercise: Here's a way to find the ideal pressure for your putting grip.

- Waggle the putterhead back and forth just above the surface of the green, first holding it as tightly as you can and then holding it as softly as you can.

- You'll find that you have a much better feel for the weight of the putterhead with the softer versus the tighter grip.

- Then roll putts starting with that very soft grip, firming it little by little until you find your ideal combination of feel and control of the putterhead.

Rehearse Your Stroke?

If you watch the pros, you'll see that some take practice strokes and some don't. Which should you do? The first option to consider is the simplest: Don't take a practice stroke. This avoids the self-consciousness and mechanical feeling that sometimes arises after making one or more practice strokes before you address the ball. Not taking practice strokes promotes a spontaneous swinging of the putter as an athletic response to what the putt looks and feels like. Just go through your routine and stroke the putt. That's what I do.

However, I sometimes make an exception and take one or two practice strokes in certain situations. For example, if I have a very fast downhill putt, I'll want to either hover the putterhead (as in the "Slick Sliders" chapter) or make a very small stroke. In that case, I may rehearse the feel of hovering and/or the size of a very small swing. Another case is a really long putt, or one from well off the green. For those I often practice the same kind of feel swing I would when chipping: rehearsing the size of the swing and the speed of the putterhead through impact.

If you do take practice strokes, you should have a specific purpose for them. Depending on the purpose they serve for your routine, I recommend you use the appropriate names to describe them: relaxing swing, feel swing, tempo swing, rhythm swing, and rehearsal swing.

A relaxing swing is used only to relax the shoulders, arms, and hands. It need not have a relationship to the size of the stroke you intend to use. A feel swing is used to get a feel for the size of the stroke you intend to make in relation to speed. A tempo swing is used to set the speed of both the back and forward parts of your stroke. A rhythm swing is used to set the sequencing and flow of the start, transition, and finish of the stroke. A rehearsal swing is used to preview the exact size, tempo, and rhythm of the stroke you intend to make.

For the relaxing and tempo purposes, it works best to swing the putter back and forth several times without stopping in between. For the feel, rhythm, and rehearsal purposes, it's important to make separate, complete putting strokes from start to finish.

Where should you make your practice strokes? One place is next to the ball, swinging parallel to the intended line of the putt. That's ideal for a rehearsal swing. For the relaxing, feel, or tempo swings, it's best to take your practice strokes behind the ball, looking past it toward the target. This is helpful for feeling the relationship between the speed of the putt and the size of the stroke.

Should there be a set number of practice strokes? The benefit of a set number is that it makes it easy to repeat your routine. However, there is the danger of becoming too rigid, to the point of superstition. It's good to keep your routine consistent, but it's also important to maintain the kind of flexibility that will allow you to take an extra swing or two if the situation and your intuition call for it.

Exercise: Experiment with not using practice strokes. Then try using practice strokes, exploring the various types, locations, and numbers of swings. Find the routine that is most comfortable and helps you to be the most consistent, and you'll *make* more putts.

Your eyes are designed to work best looking straight ahead, with both eyes at the same height and at the same distance from the object that you're looking at. That's exactly how you read a putt from behind the ball or behind the hole: looking straight ahead along the line, both eyes horizontally level and at the same distance from the hole.

But when you set up to the putt and turn your head to look down the line toward the hole, it's a different story. Your eyes are looking sideways, not straight ahead. They are tilted, one higher than the other. One is closer to the hole than the other. An all too common perceptual problem occurs in this different position: the break looks different from what you saw behind the ball. That's why I like to say that if we were really meant to play golf, we'd have eyes on each side of our ear.

The Challenge: When you have different lines for the putt in mind, two things can happen: 1) you feel doubt about the line you originally chose and don't make a committed stroke, or 2) you adjust your stroke to the other line, but it turns out to be wrong. Worse yet, sometimes you do both—you adjust to the wrong line for the putt and also make a tentative, uncommitted stroke.

The Solution: The read from behind the ball or the hole, with your eyes working the optimum way, is usually more accurate. The task is to override your perception of how the line appears from your putting stance. Make a strong commitment to the original line and trust your process of stroking the putt where the putterface is aiming. Send the ball down that line, knowing that your level-eye view from behind the ball is the more accurate one. Making a committed, positive stroke gives you the best chance to hole the putt. If you *made* your putt, but it turns out that the line you chose wasn't accurate, learn what you can from the outcome to improve your green-reading ability.

If you're ready to putt, but your doubt about the line is so strong that you feel it would be difficult to commit to that line, don't do it! Go back behind the ball and read the putt again. When you're convinced of the line, use a discolored bit of grass or part of an old pitch mark in front of the ball as an intermediate target. When you take your stance again, aim the putterface toward the intermediate target. Get your feel for speed and commit to rolling the ball over that spot.

You may prefer to use the line marked on the ball as a reference point for aim. Align the putterface to the line on the ball and commit to starting the putt in that direction.

Exercise: Whenever you practice putting, spend some time on breaking putts using your full routine. Read the putt from behind the ball, then take your stance and notice whether it now looks like there is a different break to the putt. If so, practice the process of committing to the original read of the putt. That means forcing yourself to ignore what you're seeing from your stance, to override your doubt, and to make a committed stroke along the line you saw from behind the ball. Over time you will develop the mental toughness to commit to your read and conquer your doubt about breaking putts during your round.

Aim Is the Name of the Game

As we discussed in the last chapter, a tilted, uneven view distorts your perception. When you set the putterhead behind the ball, it's not uncommon that the putterface is aimed in a different direction than it looks.

There are a number of factors that can affect your perception of alignment. Where your eyes are in relation to the ball can distort how you see the direction in which the putterface is aimed. One common error is setting up to a putt with your eyes too far inside the line. That usually causes you to aim the putterface outside the line. The reverse holds true for a stance with the eyes in a position outside the line, although that stance is far less common. Having your eyes more directly over the ball can decrease distortion, making your perceived alignment closer to your actual alignment.

How far forward or back in the stance the ball is positioned can also influence your perception. With the ball too far forward, you're likely to be aimed more inside the line than you think; too far back and you're likely to be aimed outside the line on which you intend the ball to travel.

The design of your putter, and how much the shaft is offset from the face, can also determine how well you aim. It's no accident that many modern putters are designed with built-in, high-tech alignment aids.

The Challenge: No matter how good your stroke is or how well you read a putt, if the putterface isn't aimed where you think it is, holing the putt becomes more a matter of luck than skill. The challenge is to overcome perceptual distortion so that your aim is as accurate as possible.

The Solution: Take note of how your perception of aim changes when you are closer to or farther from the ball, and when you have the ball farther forward or back in your stance. Find the ball position and stance that enable you to aim the most accurately.

Exercise: Here's how to find out where your eyes are in relation to the ball. While keeping the posture of your putting stance, drop a coin or a tee from the point directly between your eyes. Where it lands will reveal whether your eyes are directly above some part of the ball or not. Adjust your stance and repeat until you find your ideal position.

Use the line on the ball to check your aim. Before you pick up your ball mark, adjust the ball so that the line on the ball matches the starting line of your putt. As you stand behind the ball, check your aim using your puttershaft as a straightedge. With one eye closed, line up the edge of the shaft with the line on the ball, then look along the shaft toward the hole. That will show you where the line on the ball is truly pointing. Especially on relatively straight, level putts inside eight feet, using the line on the ball may give you an added feeling of certainty about your aim.

FIND THE SWEET SPOT

If you find yourself leaving putts just a bit short or pushing them ever so slightly, it may be because you're not hitting the ball with the sweet spot of the putterface.

The *sweet spot* is the point on the putterface that's in the effective center according to weight. Impact away from the sweet spot, toward the toe or heel, is actually a mis-hit, which gives the feeling and sound of a less than perfect transfer of energy from the putterhead to the ball. Most putters have a line or other mark on the top of the putterhead. The sweet spot should be straight below the mark, in the center of the putterface.

You can check the sweet spot by holding the putter near the end of the grip and letting it hang loosely. Tap the putterface in different spots from end to end. When you find a spot where the head doesn't twist to one side or the other, you're tapping the sweet spot.

The Challenge: You may be missing the sweet spot because of a surprisingly common but rarely mentioned optical illusion. Like most golfers, you try to (and probably think you do) set the sweet spot of the putter directly behind the middle of the ball. However, when you look at the putter and ball from your putting stance, the ball can actually be lined up slightly more toward the toe of the putter than it looks.

The Solution: Ask a friend to help you find out how much you're influenced by this optical illusion. Take your stance and set your putter so that it looks like the sweet spot is right behind the center of the ball. Have your friend reach between your forearms and press his or her finger down on the end of the grip to hold the putter exactly in place. Then let go of the putter. Walk around behind the putterhead and look down the line in the direction the putterface is pointing. If it looks like the ball is closer to the toe than it should be, gently move the putterhead along the ground until the sweet spot is directly behind the center of the ball.

Walk back into your stance and take your grip without moving the putter. See what it looks like to you now that the sweet spot actually is directly behind the middle of the ball. If you needed to move the putter, the ball may look as though it's a bit closer to the heel when you return to your setup position. But that's what it needs to look like if you want the ball lined up with the sweet spot.

When you swing the putter and strike the ball on the sweet spot, you'll notice a different sound, a more solid feel, and a truer roll than what you're used to. You've probably been hitting putts toward the toe of your putter for your entire golf career. Now you finally know what it feels like to hit the ball with the sweet spot of your putter.

Exercise: Line up several balls on the practice green. Play the first ball as far out toward the toe of the putter as you can and the next toward the heel. Alternate toe and heel putts, gradually moving the impact toward the sweet spot. Learning the difference in feel between a ball struck on the sweet spot and one that's not will keep you focused on setting the putterhead properly before every putt.

Every Putt Starts as a Straight Putt

> All putts are straight putts. If the contour of the green creates a
> right to left breaking putt, you aim at a point where you believe
> the ball will begin to turn toward the hole and hit the putt
> straight at that point.
>
> —Bobby Locke

It helps to think of every putt as a straight putt. Of course, not
every putt actually *is* a straight putt. The point is that you want
to swing your putter *as if* they all were. Start every putt straight
along the line you've chosen and in the direction the putterface
is aiming. Then trust that gravity (or grain) will move the ball
the way you guessed it would as it rolls toward the hole.

The Challenge: A common fault that affects even top pros is
the tendency to direct the ball at impact by pushing or pulling
the putt away from the line on which it was originally aimed.

Most golfers underestimate the amount of break in a given
putt and aim too much toward the hole. If you do this, you'll
redirect the ball further away from the hole as you swing (by
either pushing it more inside-out or pulling it more outside-in)
to give the putt more room to break. This is a response to a lack
of trust in where you've aimed the putterface, because you sense
that you haven't set up for enough break. On the occasions
when you feel that you're playing too much break, you'll also
redirect the ball at impact, this time pulling or pushing it toward the hole.

The Solution: The remedy for pushing or pulling putts is to read for maximum break and then commit to the line you've chosen. Get a feel for the swing size that will give you the speed you intend. Commit to making the same stroke you would for a straight putt, one that will send the ball where the putterface is aimed. Remember that your job is not to guide the ball into the hole. Your job is to get the ball started on its way.

Exercise: Use the line on the ball to see if your putt is rolling as it would for a straight putt. Adjust a ball so that the line on the ball matches the line that you've read for a breaking putt. Set your putterface behind the ball so that it's perpendicular to the line on the ball. Then make your stroke. Watch the line on the ball as it rolls. If the line stays sharp and steady, it means that at impact the putterface was square to the line and the swing path was moving in the right direction. If the line wobbles as the ball rolls, work on aligning the putterface square to the line and adjusting the swing path that the putterhead takes through impact. Find the alignment and swing path that make the line stay sharp. The size of your swing will change depending on distance, but the alignment and swing path for your straight-putt stroke is the one to use on every putt.

CHASE IT DOWN THE LINE

How the putter follows through after impact is important for the both the speed and the direction of the putt. In the ideal follow-through, you want to feel as though the putterhead is chasing the ball down the line. I remember watching Jack Nicklaus holing a critical putt on the 17th green in the last round of his final Masters victory in 1986. His putterhead chased the ball down the line, and he kept extending the putter toward the hole as he walked and watched his putt track into the cup.

The Challenge: A poor follow-through leads to many problematic habits. Stopping short just after impact leads to the habit of deceleration. Letting the putterhead fall to one side or the other promotes pushing or pulling. Another common habit is topping the putt, either because you've pulled your arms in or come up out of your posture at impact. That means the putt will roll a shorter distance than you expected for the stroke you made and have little chance of going in the hole.

The Solution: Chasing the ball down the line with the putterhead helps prevent all of these tendencies. Keep the putterhead moving along the line of the putt a few inches farther than you normally do. The image of chasing the ball encourages you to keep the putterhead low to the ground, with the swing path following the line of the putt.

Exercise: On the practice green, set the putterhead directly behind and touching the ball, aimed at a hole just a few feet away. Without taking a backswing, shove the ball with the putterface toward the hole. Extend the putterhead along the line after the ball is on its way and hold the finish for a second or two. Repeat this several times.

Then set up to the same putt and make a regular stroke. Focus on following through after impact with the same feeling you had when you were shoving the ball toward the hole. Again, hold your finish after you chase the ball down the line.

Apply this technique for longer putts and breaking putts. Practice until you can consistently finish your stroke the same way for any putt.

When you chase it down the line, you'll be ready to walk the putt in with your putter pointing at the hole, just like Jack did.

SECTION V

THE BEST PUTTING ROUTINE EVER

When asked how he made the incredible clutch putts he did when he was dominating the world of professional golf, Tiger Woods said, "I read the putt, I get a feel for the speed, I put a good roll on it, and then I just see what happens."

THE SECRET TO A GREAT ROUTINE

We've explored the components of *making* a putt: reading the green and choosing a line, getting a feel for the speed of the green and the pace of the putt, and making a stroke that gets the ball rolling. Now let's combine them into a great putting routine, from start to finish.

The secret to a great routine is dealing with each variable—aim, speed, and stroke—one at a time. The first step in your routine is to read the putt. Start with the overall lay of the land. See the high and low points around the green, find the fall line through the hole, and examine the last few feet of the putt. Get a clear picture of the line you think the ball will follow on its journey.

Practice strokes are next, if you take any. Now you're ready to address the ball.

Set the putter behind the ball, with the face perpendicular to your chosen starting line. For aiming, you can use an intermediate target or the line on the ball, if you find these helpful.

Take your stance and confirm that the sweet spot of the putter is behind the middle of the ball and that the putter face is aimed properly. Establish the relationship of your shoulders, arms, and hands to the puttershaft.

Say to yourself, "Done with direction," and make a commitment to send the ball on your starting line. Take a full breath, and as you exhale let a feeling of softness flow down your arms.

Now take a good long look at the distance to the hole and try to get a sense of how much uphill or downhill the slope is, and how fast or slow the green is. Focus on the full picture of the putt for at least three seconds to create a strong imprint of it in your mind. When you look back toward the ball, pause for just a moment to bring that picture to mind. With a feel for the distance in mind, commit to sending the ball into that picture. The size of the stroke is determined by your instinctive hand-eye coordination. It is an athletic response to your vision of the putt.

Make your putting-to-nowhere stroke, just as you would for a straight putt, without any push or pull, without any hitting action to it. Chase the ball down the line with the putter-head, then hold your finish. After that, turn your head to watch the ball tracking toward the hole.

If you executed your putting routine that way, you will definitely feel that you *made* your putt. Then only two things can happen—either the ball will go in the hole, or it won't. If it does, enjoy your success. If it doesn't, learn from it.

Exercise: Perhaps the most overlooked but most important thing to practice is your putting routine. Use your full routine, including your green-reading process, just as you would on the course. It may take more time, but you'll be making a very good exchange of quantity for quality. What you want to practice is flowing through your routine with regular, rhythmic tempo. Practice sessions are also an opportunity to experiment with different ways of working with your breathing and your practice stroke. If you're careful not to get sloppy or to short-circuit the process when you practice, you'll find that your routine will serve you better when you play.

DONE WITH DIRECTION

A great putting routine starts with reading your putt for line and speed. The next step is setting up to the putt in relation to the start line you've chosen.

First set the putterhead behind the ball with the face perpendicular to the start line. If you set your feet first and they're not perfectly parallel to your line, it's more difficult to aim the putterface.

Set the putterface with your eyes directly over the ball. That is the most accurate way to aim and to set the sweet spot. Then take your stance in relation to the putterface and the line.

If you take any practice strokes, you'll need to reconnect to the line before you set up to the putt. That's why I favor either not taking practice strokes, or doing so behind the ball. It's easier to stay connected to the starting line of the putt when you're walking into address from behind the ball than when you're setting up to the putt after taking practice strokes next to the ball.

Once you're in your stance, let your eyes follow the line of the putt from the putterface to the hole. It's important that you feel committed to your starting line. As we discussed in an earlier chapter, the read sometimes looks different when you get into your stance. If you don't feel committed to your original read, take the time to go back and determine the line again from behind the ball. You can use an intermediate target or the line on the ball to anchor your commitment.

When you've taken your stance and feel fully committed to your line, say to yourself: "Done with direction," or "Got the line." At that point you are committed to starting the putt in the direction the putterface is aiming, *no matter what*. You need to be done with any concern about the line so that you can focus only on speed and stroke.

If you're still thinking about the line, perhaps because you have doubts about the break or your aim, you won't be able to tune in to the feel for distance and probably won't make a committed stroke. If you have some difficulty figuring out the break, you can become so absorbed in thinking about the line that you forget about speed and stroke. You leave the putt short and find yourself saying, "I fell in love with the line and forgot to hit the putt."

When you say, "Done with direction," you really have to mean it. Say it with a feeling of conviction. Giving those words lip service without really being committed to the line leaves you open to last-second doubts that can cause you to push or pull the putt at impact.

Being done with direction is essential for *making* the putt. When you set your putter and take your stance, you need to make a clear commitment to the line and your aim, and a clear end to the concern about either of those. If you can't, then get out of your stance, reread the putt, reset your aim, and recommit to being done with direction.

Exercise: Practice putting with your full routine and saying the words "Done with direction" out loud, until it becomes second nature and an essential part of your routine.

IMPRINT THE DISTANCE

You've aimed the putter and taken your stance. You've made the commitment to starting the ball on your chosen line, in the direction the putterface is pointing, by saying, "Done with direction." Now it's time to turn your attention to speed.

As we discussed earlier, a feel for speed is based on hand-eye coordination. The best way to get a feel for speed is by taking a good long look at the target.

Using that long look at the target to imprint the distance in your mind is an important component in your routine. It helps sustain your connection to the target from the time you look back toward the ball until you've completed your putting stroke.

Many golfers take several quick glances between the ball and the hole before stroking their putt. Sometimes their eyes go back and forth so many times and so quickly it's as if they're trying to see the hole and the ball at the same time.

Actually, you *can* see the hole and the ball at the same time. Your sense of sight, the part of your brain that processes visual images, gets input from two sources. One source, obviously, is your eyes. The other is your memory. When one of those is the main source of visual imagery, the other fades into the background. That's what happens when you daydream: Your eyes are open, but your mind is somewhere else.

How clearly you can recall a picture of the distance you want to send the ball depends on how strongly you imprint in your mind what you see when you look at the line and the hole. That's why you take a good long look once you're "done with direction."

Focus on the length of the putt and how uphill or downhill it is. Include grain in your overall sense of the speed of the green. Look at the putt for at least three seconds, imprinting the whole picture in your memory. When you look down toward the ball, take a moment to recollect that picture, to see it as clearly as you can in your mind's eye.

Once you have that picture in mind, you're ready to stroke the putt. Your feel for speed comes from your instinctive hand-eye coordination, an athletic response to the target. The clearer your picture, the better your speed will be.

Exercise: Practice switching the focus of your visual perception from your eyes to your memory, particularly in relation to distance. Turn your head to one side and look at an object across the room for several seconds. Then turn back and look straight ahead. Bring to mind, as vividly as you can, the picture of what you were just seeing, especially how far away the object was. Hold it in your mind's eye as long as you can. Repeat until the shift of your visual focus from your eyes to your memory is easily done.

Once you've trained yourself to bring the picture from memory to mind, the "Guessing Game for Feel" exercise (see page 35) will help you train your hand-eye coordination. Look at the distance to the fringe for three seconds. Then look down at the ball, take a moment to recollect the picture of what you saw, and stroke your putt to the target you see in your mind's eye. Practice this way and you'll improve your feel for speed in response to your visual image.

Roll It into the Picture

You've taken a good long look to imprint the distance in your mind. You've turned back toward the ball and brought the memory, the picture of that distance, to the forefront of your mind. Now it's time to roll the putt into the picture.

Your instinctive hand-eye coordination determines the size of the stroke you'll make to give the putt the proper speed in response to your sense of the distance.

The visual input is from your memory rather than from your eyes, but the hand-eye coordination works the same way. It's still action in response to what you're seeing.

To make a smooth, free stroke, let a feeling of softening and relaxation flow down your shoulders and arms to your hands, dissolving any tightness that may be there. You may find it helpful to do so as you let out a full breath. It only takes a second, and you can do this just before or after taking your long look to imprint the picture of the distance into your memory. It's as if you're settling in to your commitment to the putt in both body and mind.

When you're ready, roll the ball into the picture with your putting-to-nowhere stroke. It's the stroke you would make for the start of a straight putt, using the up and down movement of your front shoulder to keep the putterhead on line through impact, without any pushing or pulling.

If you're really focused on rolling it into the picture, you'll feel your awareness and your energy directed more toward the target than toward the ball. This encourages the feeling of sending the ball toward the target rather than hitting at the ball, which promotes the action of the putterhead chasing the ball down the line.

Exercise: Stand on the practice green about twenty feet from a hole. Without a putter, hold one ball in your hand and place another in front of your feet, where it would normally be when you putt. Take your putting stance, and then turn your head and take a good long look at the distance to the hole. After a few seconds, look down toward the ball in front of your feet. Bring to the forefront of your mind the image of the distance you were seeing. When you have the image in mind, toss the ball underhand into the picture without looking up. Your first toss may come up short. Most people are a bit tentative when performing this unfamiliar exercise. After one or two more tosses you'll start to trust your hand-eye coordination and get better results.

Then practice the same sequence with your putter. Experiment with how long you have to look to imprint the distance, how long it takes to bring the image to mind, and how long after that you initiate the action of rolling the ball. Find a rhythm that is comfortable, one that lets you do each component thoroughly without feeling like you're taking too long. That will be the rhythm of your best putting routine.

Hold Your Finish

With commitment to the line and a feel for the speed, you've made the size stroke you wanted and sent the ball on its way from the sweet spot of the putterface. You've chased the ball down the line with your putterhead.

How you complete the stroke is another important part of your routine, and the best way to do that is to *hold your finish*.

Holding your finish means leaving the putterhead in position for a second or two after it has reached its furthest extension forward in the stroke. When you hold the finish, the position gives you information about the direction in which the putterhead was moving and where the putterface was pointing. It will also tell you if you maintained the capital *Y* shape made at address by your arms, hands, and the puttershaft.

If you pushed or pulled the putt away from the line you originally chose, you'll be able to see that by the way you finish the stroke. If you turned the putterface through impact, or bent your wrists, you'll be able to see that as well. You'll know if you need to improve your commitment to the line or the steadiness of your stroke.

Holding your finish also has another benefit. When you know in the back of your mind that you'll be accountable for the quality of your stroke, you'll make a better one. You'll do your best to produce the optimum stroke needed to get to a good finish. That will promote a good swing path and impact position, and will keep you from pushing or pulling the putt.

When you hold your finish and feel that you *made* your putt, then you know that if your putt missed the hole it was because of an incorrect guess about the break or the speed. Now you have an opportunity to improve your reading ability. Most amateurs miss on the low side of the hole because they under-estimate the amount of break. When you hold your finish you can learn to play enough break to stay on the high side, and that means holing more putts.

Exercise: At the end of the forward motion of the putting stroke, some golfers tend to recoil, or bring the putter back quickly toward the center of their stance. If you have this habit, it will be difficult to hold your finish at the end of the forward motion of the putterhead. To break the habit, practice holding your finish for an exaggerated length of time. Finish the forward stroke and hold the putter in place for three full seconds before you move it.

A vitally important point, especially on the through-swing, is keeping your head down and still. Look at the ball's original position until the ball itself vanishes from sight. If your head moves, everything is for naught. My head eventually turns to let me watch what is happening to the ball, but it swivels and never sways forward.

—Bobby Locke

You've made your stroke and held your finish. The next step in the routine is a subtle but important one: It's the way you watch the putt roll out.

For the hands, arms, and shoulders to work together properly, it's essential to maintain your head position and spine angle until the ball is well on its way. This element of putting is so important that during his final Masters victory, Jack Nicklaus told his caddie (his eldest son Jackie) to remind him before every single putt to keep his head steady.

The Challenge: If you want to watch the putt as it rolls out, your head will instinctively lift up so that your eyes can be horizontal, the position from which they work the best. It's natural for your body to follow your head. So if you start to look by lifting your head, your body will come up out of your putting stance, and your spine angle will change.

You come up out of your stance because you want to know how the putt is doing. In anticipation, you start looking—peeking—earlier and earlier in the stroke, until you look up even before the putterhead impacts the ball. If you come up out of your stance before impact, it's unlikely that you'll make solid contact.

The Solution: The best way to ensure that you don't come up out of your putting stance is to just turn your head to track the roll of your putt. Let the stroke finish, then *turn to track*.

You can train yourself to do this in two stages. First, practice rolling putts while keeping your eyes focused on the spot where the ball was. Instead of looking, just listen for the sound of the ball falling into the hole. Start with very short putts and then gradually increase the length of putts you're practicing.

The second stage is practicing when and how to turn your head. Keep your head steady with your eyes looking toward the spot where the ball was until you hold the finish of your stroke. After you have held that finish for a second, simply rotate your head toward the target—don't lift it—keeping your spine angle stable. Your chin should follow a line parallel to the start line of the putt, just as your left shoulder did in the through stroke. You will be able to see the finish of the putt without changing your spine angle.

That's how you turn your head to track and follow the roll of the ball. It keeps you from coming up out of the putt, even when you're eager to see the outcome. Putt this way and you'll see more of your putts tracking into the hole.

BE AN OBJECTIVE DETECTIVE

Every putt is a learning opportunity. After every putt leaves the putterface, the first thing that you need to reflect on is the quality of execution.

If the putt went well, you know it and you have the opportunity to reinforce your process and deepen the extent to which your routine is consistent and your stroke ingrained. If the putt didn't go well, take time to reflect on your stroke and your routine, and how they could have been better.

It's important to clear whatever negative emotions arise about the outcome of the putt by taking one or more deep breaths. That's because insight and learning can't happen in the midst of emotional upheaval. Instead, calm down and examine the evidence like a good detective, one who is unemotional and objective. This will allow you to find clues and learn from them.

If you *made* the putt and holed the putt, reinforce your success by giving yourself credit for a job well done. Build your confidence with a two-part sentence. The first part is a self-compliment about your ability: "That's how I always putt . . ." The second part reinforces your process ". . . when I roll it into the picture." Other examples are, "That's how I always putt when I commit to being done with direction," or "That's how I always stroke it when I feel like I'm putting to nowhere."

It's good to reinforce success on challenging putts that barely miss, or long putts that come so close that you wouldn't want a do-over.

If you *make* your putt but don't hole it, learn from it by being an objective detective. If you get angry or frustrated over the outcome, you need to take a full, slow breath to calm yourself down. Feel good about having *made* your putt. Don't be a perfectionist. If it was a long putt and it almost went in, it's unrealistic to expect much more.

If your read was wrong, examine the evidence like an objective detective to discover what you misjudged about the slope or speed of the green. When you respond this way, you can learn from every putt and continually improve your green-reading skills.

If you don't *make* the putt, ask yourself what was off. Was it the line? The speed? Or was it the stroke? If you felt it wasn't a good stroke, reflect on what might have gotten in the way. If you felt the stroke was good but the putt was off line, check to see if you had the putterface aimed in a different direction than you thought. If you felt like you made the swing size you intended but the ball didn't roll at the speed you thought it would, reflect on whether you took into account the slope, grain, or speed of the green.

If you made a poor stroke, chances are your speed was off as well. An overly tight grip or a lack of commitment can cause you to hit harder or to hold back instead of making a smooth stroke. Off-center contact or deceleration will also affect your speed. Whether you hold back or give it something extra, chances are the putt won't start at the speed you intended.

Develop the habit of reacting less emotionally to a poor putt. Instead of being frustrated, be an objective detective who regards every situation as another opportunity to learn. That's the best way to continually improve your putting. And when you *make* your putt, give yourself a compliment on how well you did your routine. That's the best way to build confidence.

SECTION VI

THAT ONE LOOKS A LITTLE TRICKY

Ben Hogan had a little mind game he played during one-on-one matches. He would concede every three-foot putt his opponent faced until late in the round. At that point his opponent, assuming another concession was coming, would bend down to pick up his ball. But Hogan would say, "Hang on. That one looks a little tricky." Having not putted a short putt all day, the opponent would often become unnerved and succumb to the pressure.

THE SECRET TO
MAKING CHALLENGING PUTTS

The more familiar you are with a variety of challenging putts, the more comfortable you'll be when you encounter them on the course, and the better chance you'll have of *making* them. Remember, that doesn't mean they'll all go in. You can *make* a challenging putt but not hole it. If you recognize the best putt to attempt, *make* the putt you intended and then don't hole it, you'll still usually have an easy second putt.

Steep sidehill putts for which you need to judge a combination of speed and line are especially challenging. Practice putting across a slope to explore how much the putt breaks. Correctly predicting how the ball is going to react as it rolls up, down, and across slopes only comes from extensive experience.

Other difficult putts that you should spend time practicing include two-tiered putts, putts that go up over a mound or ridge and then down again toward the hole, and putts that go down a swale and then up again toward the hole.

Many practice putting greens don't have tiers and mounds and swales, but you can think outside the box and find a way to practice on real greens that have those features. If you can get permission, go out on the course in the late afternoon or early evening to practice challenging putts.

It's also helpful to spend time practicing putting from off the green. I rarely see that practiced, yet almost everyone encounters an opportunity at least once each round. Experiment with what works best for different lies. Are you more consistent with your putter or your wedge? Does putting with a hybrid or fairway club work for you? If you can't do so on the course or the putting green, practice these shots around the short-game-area green.

Finally, spend time in practice or warm-ups rolling long putts of forty feet or more. You'll probably have one or two of these in every round, and practicing them will improve the hand-eye coordination you need to roll the ball a long distance on the green.

Exercise: The best putting practice is to practice the way you play—in a competitive situation. Find a friend for putting contests and play for a little something to add to the pressure so that you really feel the competitive edge. It doesn't have to be monetary; you can keep track of your record for bragging rights or even a year-end trophy. You can also have competitions against yourself to keep your putting sharp.

PUTTING UNDER PRESSURE

When you're playing your best, putting seems simple. You see the line, go through your routine, stroke each putt with the same rhythm, and get to watch a lot of them fall into the hole. Then you realize that this four-footer on 18 is for your best round ever. Or your playing partner asks, "Isn't this putt for your third birdie in a row? Have you ever done that before?" Now you feel pressure, and everything changes. The outcome has become a big deal—your putt is *for something*. So instead of focusing on your process for *making* the putt, you're thinking about the outcome—holing it or missing it.

Jack Nicklaus, Bobby Jones, and Tiger Woods earned reputations as the best clutch putters of all time because of their ability to stay completely focused in pressure situations. They seemed to become even more committed to their process when they were under pressure. That kind of focus enabled them to hole a lot of critical putts.

For most golfers, however, thinking about what a putt is *for* causes them to lose focus on their process. Whether it's a two-dollar weekend Nassau, the club championship, or the Masters, the pressure of a putt that is *for* something can interfere with their ability to *make* the putt, and actually lessen their chances of holing the putt.

The Challenge: Once you've made a big deal about the results, you become a self-conscious perfectionist rather than just trusting yourself to do your best. The hope of success and the fear of failure make you anxious and tense. Instead of focusing on what you need to do to roll a good putt, you start thinking about what you need to do to avoid missing. You try too hard, and you become overly analytical in your read and mechanical in your stroke.

The Solution: As soon as you hear yourself (or someone else) say, "This putt is *for* something," the alarms should go off! Act as if you were your own coach, telling yourself, "This is a ball, a few feet of grass, and a hole, and you've made plenty of these little putts." Replace the thoughts about holing or missing the putt with attention to the steps in your regular putting routine.

Anxiety makes your mind race and your body tense up. You feel uptight. So you need to slow down your mind and settle down your body before a pressure putt. Take a full, deep breath and let it out slowly. Feel the tension from your body dissolving and imagine your weight pressing your feet firmly against the ground. Take your time as you move through your routine, and then roll the putt when you feel settled and ready. You've given yourself the best chance to hole the putt, and you've gained the confidence that you can stay focused under pressure.

Exercise: Practice this "Pressure Drill" to develop mental toughness. Putt two-footers from all four directions around a hole, then do the same for three-footers, four-footers, and so on. The pressure comes from this additional rule: you have to start over if you miss a putt. See how far into the sequence you get, and with each practice session see if you can improve your record. Knowing that you can hole many short putts in a row will give you an edge in confidence when you face a pressure putt late in a match.

TURN KNEE-KNOCKERS
INTO TAP-INS

A senior golfer came to me for a putting lesson. He told me he had been a fighter pilot, but that nothing scared him as much as "a slick, downhill, left-to-right four-footer on the 18th green for all the marbles." That's why we call pressure putts like that "knee-knockers"—your knees are knocking together from fear.

The Challenge: You might have a tendency to be extra careful with pressure-packed short putts. Your stroke becomes tentative, carefully guiding the ball rather than making a confident swing. The ball just wobbles along toward the hole and barely goes in—if you're lucky.

Or you might be so fearful of missing that all you care about is getting the putt over with. You rush through your routine, take a little jab at it, and moan when the ball doesn't even sniff the hole.

You may get the bright idea to hit it hard and jam it into the cup in order to take away any break. But if you miss the hole or the putt lips out, you might be left with another knee-knocker.

The Solution: To feel less pressure when faced with a four-foot knee-knocker, turn it into a tap-in.

Few golfers worry about an eight-inch tap-in putt. Just step up, square your putter face, and make a simple little stroke. The tap-in often represents a golfer's best stroke. The putterhead moves straight back and straight through the ball with the face square at impact. It chases the ball nearly to the hole, and the ball dives into the middle of the cup at a good speed.

Your tap-in stroke is a natural swing with no guiding for direction, no concern about distance, no tension from fear of missing. You may be surprised to discover that a ball struck by your tap-in stroke will reach a hole several feet away. That's the secret to turning a knee-knocker into a tap-in.

Set up with the putterface square to the start line of the putt. Imagine that there is a hole just eight inches in front of your ball on the line toward the actual hole. Get settled, and then make the same stroke you would if you were just hitting a tap-in to that imaginary hole. The key is to follow through well past the ball, just as you would on your tap-in to a real hole. Watch as the ball rolls past your imaginary hole and into the actual hole. You just turned a four-foot knee-knocker into a tap-in!

Exercise: On the practice green, find the outline of an old hole that is a little less than four feet from one of the actual holes. Set your ball eight inches behind the outline of the hole plug, so that the line of the putt to the actual hole runs through the center of the outline. Set up to the ball and make your tap-in stroke toward the center of the hole plug. The ball should roll across the outline and into the hole. Practice this to get a feeling for a tap-in stroke that rolls the ball the right speed for a four-foot putt. Once you get comfortable with this technique, use it on the course. It's a great feeling to hear your opponent describing a four-foot putt as a knee-knocker while you are seeing it as a tap-in.

A steep, downhill putt presents an interesting dilemma. You want to make a smooth, complete stroke, but if you give the putt even a little too much speed, it could run well past the hole. How do you prevent that but still make a good stroke?

The Challenge: You know that the size of the swing that you would ordinarily make for the distance you face will send the ball far beyond the hole. Therefore, you either decelerate as you approach impact or you make a very small stroke, just a tiny jab at the ball. The ball then wobbles down the slope, off line right from the start, with poor distance control.

The Solution: Hover the putterhead off the ground so that the bottom edge of the putterface is even with the middle of the ball. Contacting the ball with the bottom edge of the face instead of the sweet spot in the center deadens the impact. This accomplishes the goal of reducing the amount of energy imparted from your ordinary stroke.

I favor hovering the putter rather than the more common approach of deadening the impact by hitting the ball well out toward the toe of the putter. When the impact is off-center toward the toe, the putterhead can turn and send the putt off the intended line. When you hover the putter, the ball is still centered on the sweet spot in relation to heel and toe of the putterhead; it's just below it on the face.

Hovering the putterhead allows you to make your ordinary stroke for the length of putt you face. You'll feel more comfortable and therefore less tense. Your stroke will naturally be more fluid, and you won't worry about the ball going too fast for that steep, downhill putt.

This technique is also useful in other situations. If you're comfortable hovering the putter, your stroke is less likely to get caught by the grass when putting from just off the green, or when the ball comes to rest against the fringe.

For downhill putts longer than ten feet or so, an alternative technique that uses your regular putting stroke is preferable. Find a spot on your line part way to the hole and make the stroke that you would for a putt of that length if it were on level ground. For example, a downhill putt of ten feet might only require the speed you'd give to a level four-foot putt. For a very fast downhill twenty-foot putt, the stroke you'd make for a six-footer could be plenty. A slick six-footer might only need your tap-in stroke, as we discussed in the previous chapter.

You may hear a caddie suggest that you "give it 50 percent" for a downhill putt. That means to roll it at the speed you would for a level putt that's half the distance of the downhill putt you're facing.

Exercise: Because it's an unfamiliar feeling not to ground your putter, it's important to practice hovering the putter until your stroke is consistent and you're comfortable enough to use it during a round. On the practice green, find a hole on a steep slope. From above the hole, practice hovering the putter, higher and higher, until you find the ideal height to make your stroke and have the ball roll at the speed you desire. Practice this and you'll feel more confident when you find yourself facing that steep downhill putt to save your par.

COMEBACKERS

You hit a downhill putt that runs well past the cup. You need to hole the next one to avoid a three-putt, but it's hard to make the commitment to hit the *comebacker* putt with enough speed to reach the hole, let alone be going fast enough to hold its line. You know how this story usually ends.

The Challenge: What makes a comebacker so difficult? You just got feedback that the ball rolled farther than you thought it would with the stroke you made. Your anxiety increased as the ball rolled farther and farther past the hole. In your mind (and sometimes out loud) you were screaming, "OH NO! THAT WAS TOO HARD!" On the next putt, your comebacker, it's tough to make a firm, committed stroke to send the ball into the back of the cup with that thought lingering in your mind.

Also, three-putting is bad enough, but you *really* don't want to have the ball go so far past the hole on the comebacker that you leave yourself another tricky downhill putt and risk a *four-putt*! Even if you take the putter back far enough, it's hard to swing through freely. Instead, you hold back and decelerate at impact.

The Solution: You need to clear the last putt completely from your memory and treat the uphill comebacker as if it were your first putt. The only thing that's helpful to keep in mind from the previous putt is what break you saw, if any, after the ball rolled past the hole. That should tell you what you need to know to read the comebacker.

It's important to visualize the image of how you want the ball to go into the hole. On the downhill putt, you pictured the ball just trickling over the front edge. This time you want to imagine the ball pouring firmly into the middle. At that speed it will hold its line and not go too far past the hole if it misses. Although it's tempting to picture it popping into the back of the cup, it's not easy to commit to that speed without worrying about it going too far by.

Go through your routine just as you would for any uphill putt, with the same sequence and rhythm. Set the putterface and take your stance. Picture the ball pouring into the middle of the hole. With that picture in mind, make your putting-to-nowhere stroke. Chase the ball down the line and hold your finish. *Make* your putt that way and you've given yourself the best chance to hole that comebacker.

Exercise: Another technique for an uphill comebacker is to putt to a spot a foot or two past the hole on the through line. Practice six-foot comebackers by sticking a tee in the green on the through line of an uphill putt one or two feet past the hole. Make the tee the target for your putt instead of the hole. If your putt is traveling at a speed that would reach the tee, when it crosses the hole, in it will go!

REALLY LONG PUTTS

> I always tell people to spend more time rolling fifty-footers. Every time I practiced putting, I finished the session by rolling a couple dozen fifty-foot putts. There's just no substitute for the feel you get from that practice.
>
> —Jerry Barber, PGA Champion

Most golfers don't practice really long putts, because they aren't a whole lot of fun to practice. They hardly ever go in the hole, and you don't get many repetitions—you roll a few putts and have to walk all the way to the other side of the green before you get to putt again.

The Challenge: To send the ball a long distance across the green requires a much bigger stroke than you usually practice. Because of that, it's hard to have confidence in your feel for the speed of a really long putt.

Taking an extra big stroke with your putter is unfamiliar, and therefore uncomfortable. Also, when you make that kind of stroke with your putter, it's necessary to get your legs and core muscles involved, the way you would when you're chipping.

The Solution: Use your chipping stroke with your putter for really long putts.

You are used to long chips across the green. If you miss the green with your approach shot after aiming to the wide side, you'll likely play a long, running chip with a mid-iron for your next shot. The ball carries the short distance over the rough and fringe, and then rolls the rest of the way, just like a long putt.

You have experience with the feel for speed when using a 7- or 8-iron to chip across the green.

The technique for putting with a chipping swing is simple. Hold the putter with the same grip you use for chipping, and set up to the ball the way you would for a long, running chip with your mid-iron. The ball can be in the middle or even slightly back in your stance, and your feet can be open to the target. You can even lean toward the target a little, so that a bit more of your weight is on your forward foot. Swing the putter as if you were chipping with your mid-iron, but make more of a sweeping stroke than one that hits down on the ball. Let your torso and legs move naturally through the swing, just as you would for a chip. Hold your finish as you do in your regular putting stroke and turn your head to track the putt. You may be surprised at how good your feel is for long putts when you use your chipping swing.

Exercise: Emulate PGA Champion Jerry Barber and spend the end of every practice session with a dozen putts of fifty feet or more. Try using your chipping swing for a few long putts, and see if it gives you better results than your regular putting stroke. Whichever way you putt them, practicing really long putts will give you confidence when you face them on the course.

UP TIERS, DOWN TIERS

Your approach shot has reached the green, but when you get to your ball you see that the hole is on a different level, and there's a steep slope you have to deal with. Now, instead of thinking about the possibility of one-putting, you're worried about three-putting.

The Challenge: Every two-tiered putt has three sections: a relatively level portion, a steep uphill or downhill slope, and then another relatively level portion. The challenge is that you have to judge two or even three different speeds for one putt.

The danger when putting down to a lower tier is getting "too cute" with the first putt—trying to be perfect, to make it just barely roll over the edge of the upper tier. If it doesn't get there, you wasted a shot, because you still have to putt down the steep slope.

Putting to an upper tier can be more challenging. If you don't make a big enough stroke, the ball won't make it to the top, and may roll all the way back to you. If you guard against being short and give it too much speed, the ball will go zooming past the hole.

Also, a steep upslope can make it look as though the top tier is flat, when in fact it continues uphill. You may be surprised that after the ball clears the rise, it stops well before you expect it to.

The Solutions

Down the Tier: Read the putt backward from the hole on the lower tier to the base of the slope, finding the point where it needs to leave the slope to roll on a line toward the hole. Then see where it needs to roll over the edge of the upper tier to get to that spot at the base. Roll the putt that will take you to that point on the edge, with just enough pace for the slope to send the ball across the lower tier to the hole.

Don't try to be perfect. Having a level ten-foot comebacker after your first putt is better than leaving it on the top tier for your second putt. Be sure to give it enough speed to get over the edge, then deal with whatever you get on the lower tier.

Up the Tier: When putting to an upper tier, the combination of line and speed requires extra attention. The first portion of the putt on the lower tier will not be subject to much break because it will be moving pretty quickly. The more it slows down on the way up, the more the slope will affect it. Imagine the putt rolling from the foot of the hill across the slope to the spot where it goes over the top edge. From there you can read it to roll out as a level or slightly uphill putt would.

As for the speed of an uphill two-tiered putt, it's the same as the speed you'd need for an evenly sloping uphill putt from the ball to the hole. The average of the speeds you need for the two flat sections and the steep slope is the same speed as a putt of equal length that is steadily climbing uphill all the way to the hole.

In your routine, after reading the sections of the two-tiered putt, set up and take a good long look at the hole, imagining an evenly sloping uphill putt of that distance and steepness. Then roll your putt into that picture.

It's not a sight you like to see: You come up to the green and there's your ball, on the fringe, resting against the collar of the first cut of rough.

The Challenge: This shot is particularly challenging because the putterhead can get caught in the thick grass. If that happens as you take the putter back, it can disrupt the rhythm and tempo of your stroke and cause a mis-hit. On the through swing, if grass gets between the putterface and the ball, it can deaden the impact. Worse yet, really thick grass can nearly stop the putterhead altogether, causing you to stub the putt and barely move the ball.

The Solution: There are a number of techniques that will prevent the grass from interfering with the putterface during the stroke.

I prefer the "pop-putt" technique: Hit sharply down on the ball with the face of the putter, which causes the ball to pop a little way into the air before rolling toward the hole.

Set up with the ball very far back in your stance, well behind your back foot. Your hands need to be held low and forward of the middle of your stance, so that the putterface tilts down, as much as forty-five degrees from vertical. Using your wrists without moving the grip part of the putter backward, lift the putterhead sharply and then bang it down on the ball at a very steep angle. The ball will bounce off the ground and pop into the air with topspin. When the ball lands it will zip along the green toward the hole.

Another technique is not to use a putter at all, but to "belly" a wedge instead. That means hitting the middle, or belly, of the ball with the leading edge of one of your wedges. This takes some practice and precision—if the wedge hits the ball too high, you'll top the ball and not get the speed you're looking for; hit it too low and the wedge will slip under the ball and give it backspin, which also reduces the distance it will roll. Once you're able to strike the ball solidly in the middle, you need to develop your feel for speed with the wedge.

There is another outside-the-box technique, but be cautioned that if you miss, it's likely to be a bad miss. This method involves turning the putter 90 degrees in your hand and using the toe of the putter to hit the ball. The toe, like the edge of the wedge, goes through the grass with less resistance than the face of the putter. This only works with a blade-style putter that has a relatively small, flat toe.

Try the different methods in practice to determine which ones give you the most consistent results. Keep in mind that you need to put in the time to practice these techniques before you can use them with confidence on the course.

PUTT OUTSIDE THE BOX

When the ball is just a few feet off the green, you may wonder whether you should putt or chip. If you putt, the thicker grass might send the ball off line or interfere with the speed. Chipping gets the ball over the rough, but it brings in the risk of a mis-hit. How do you decide?

Arnold Palmer's maxim for a shot from just off the green was, "An average putt is going to get as close as a good chip," so he usually chose the putter. For modern pros, with the quality and variety of wedges available to them, there's a different rule of thumb. It's still true that if you want to play the safest shot possible and leave the ball closest to the hole, you should putt. But if you're trying to hole it and are willing to risk being a bit farther from the hole if you miss, you should chip. Remember that this is for players who have excellent technique and equipment, and who practice a lot.

It's usually safer to putt whenever you can. There's a chance that you'll mis-hit a delicate chip, especially from a tight lie. You might stub the club into the ground or blade the ball across the green. If you can get the putter on the ball without grass getting in the way and there aren't obstacles in front of you, you should putt.

How do you know how big a stroke to make when you're a few feet or more off the green? The ball rolls fastest for the first few feet of the putt, so the longer grass of the fairway or fringe won't slow the ball down as much as you think, unless you're going across a long stretch of it. Your instinct from looking at the shaggier surface will be to make a slightly bigger swing than you would for the same putt on the green. That's generally a sufficient adjustment. Don't outthink yourself and hit it too much harder than you would a regular putt.

What about other clubs? Experimentation is the key. Go to the short-game area with all of your clubs. Find out what feels most comfortable under different conditions. How far off the green are you comfortable putting? Try other clubs for this type of shot, especially hybrids or fairway metals. Choose the club that you can swing with the most confidence and that gives you the most consistent results.

Many golfers assume that if the ball is farther from the green than the fringe, they can't putt. Don't assume—think outside the box and find out for yourself. See what you can do with a putter across a variety of ground conditions and from a variety of distances. If you're playing links golf as they do in Scotland, there's almost no limit as to how far from the green you can use your putter. It's not uncommon to see players putt from fifty yards away in the Open Championship on a windy day!

SECTION VII

GETTING BETTER ALL THE TIME

They say I'm lucky. I agree, and then explain that the more I practice, the luckier I get.

—Gary Player

The Secret to Continuous Improvement

Putting is like wisdom: partly a natural gift and partly the accumulation of experience.

—Arnold Palmer

You can improve your putting while you play by using a cycle of continuous improvement. It is based on the *PAR Approach* that I introduced in *Zen Golf: Mastering the Mental Game*. *PAR* stands for "Preparation, Action, and Response" to results. By applying these in the proper sequence, you establish a feedback loop for performance that lets you get better as you play. Prepare the best you can, act as effectively as possible, and then review the results to see what you can learn. If you have success, reinforce the effective preparation and action you brought to bear. If the results were unsatisfactory, adjust your next preparation or action, based on what you learned from an analysis of the outcome. That will give you the best chance for improved performance in the execution of the next putt.

Preparation requires clarity, commitment, and composure. Do a thorough job of reading the green. See clearly how you expect the ball to track toward the hole. Commit to both the line and speed you chose. Focus on *making* the putt as your task. Compose yourself, using your breathing to dissolve tension so that you feel settled and grounded as you address the putt.

Action is performing your routine, following the process for *making* your putt. Set up for and commit to your aim, trust your feel for speed, get the ball started on line with a good stroke—and then let the ball do its job to find the hole. Action is letting your body respond to the picture of the putt in your mind's eye and making a smooth and rhythmic stroke without pushing, pulling, or holding back.

Response to results helps you reinforce successes and learn from mistakes. Then you can make any adjustments necessary to prepare for the next action. If you *made* your putt, whether or not it went in the hole, say something positive like, "I love the way I rolled that one," or "That's the way I always roll it when I commit to my line and make a free-flowing stroke." If you made the putt but it was off line or off speed, learn from it— read the putt over again and ask yourself, "What did I miss in the first read that affected the line and speed?" In that way you can use an incorrectly read putt as an opportunity to improve your green-reading ability.

If you didn't feel like you *made* your putt, reflect on what got in the way. Was it your preparation: Did you not have enough clarity in your read or enough commitment to the line and speed? Was it your stroke: Did you have inconsistent grip pressure, not chase the ball down the line, or not hold your finish? Reflect on what you could have done differently in your preparation or stroke, and establish a strong intention to do a better job on your next putt.

Don't waste a poor putt—learn from it!

GET OUT OF YOUR OWN WAY

> Bad putting is due more to the effect the green has upon the player than it has upon the action of the ball.
>
> —Bobby Jones

I remember watching a playoff at the Masters where a golfer had a short, slightly downhill putt to win. As he looked at the putt from this side and that, the television commentator said, "Oh no, he's taking much longer to read this putt than he does in his regular routine. That's not a good sign." And it wasn't.

The Challenge: Getting in your own way is the opposite of being in the Zone. When you doubt your intuition or abilities, you invite tension and self-consciousness. When you're overly concerned about results, you don't trust your regular process. Whenever you try too hard, try to be perfect, or overthink the putt, you're getting in your own way.

When it comes to reading a putt, if you have doubt about what you're seeing, you might look at it for too long and over-analyze the break. You might see breaks that aren't there—sometimes a putt is just a straight putt. You may start seeing so many possibilities that you lose track of what you saw in the first place. The great Bobby Jones said, "I have never been able to see more rolls and bumps in a minute than I could in five seconds."

When it comes to speed, you may start thinking about what could go wrong, either leaving the putt short or hitting it too far by. Then you get in your own way by overdoing the opposite. If your last thought is, "Don't leave this one short," you'll run it six feet by. If you're afraid of the speed of the green, you'll decelerate at impact and leave it short. If you "fall in love with the line," thinking only about direction, you'll completely lose your focus on speed.

When it comes to the stroke, if you've pushed or pulled a couple of putts, you may start thinking about your technique and mechanics. You might fiddle with your grip, your swing path, or your ball position. If there's doubt in your mind about how you're swinging the putter, you're likely to make a tentative, guiding, or jabbing stroke.

The ultimate expression of getting in your own way is the yips. The yips are marked by tremendous anxiety about your results with no confidence in your ability. If you have the yips, there's a chapter for you at the end of this book.

The Solution: Whenever you find yourself reading a putt for too long or thinking too much about the mechanics of your stroke, do your best to stop what you're doing and start fresh. My Buddhist teacher liked to say, "First thought, best thought," which is the opposite of second-guessing yourself. Turn your back to the putt and take a deep breath. Then take a fresh look. Whatever your first guess is for the line of your putt, commit to that. When you get out of your own way, you give yourself the best chance to *make* the putt, and you give the ball the best chance to go into the hole.

Stick to your routine. Just focus on the things you need to do to *make* your putt. Remember: once the ball has started to roll, the outcome is beyond your control.

SKILLS PRACTICE VERSUS PERFORMANCE PRACTICE

Throughout this book you've been given exercises that you can use to practice your putting. It's important when planning a practice session to distinguish between skills practice and performance practice.

Skills Practice: In skills practice, you isolate various parts of the putting process and work on each one repetitively. You don't need to do your full routine for each putt. For example, when working on your putting-to-nowhere stroke, roll ball after ball until you feel like your stroke flows smoothly, you're making sweet spot impact, and you have a good follow-through. Another example of skills practice is to set up several balls in a row, each with a line across the top, and practice stroking them so that the line stays sharp. You can practice the "Guessing Game for Feel" (see page 35) or the "Leapfrog Drill" (see page 39) for your hand-eye coordination in judging speed. All of these exercises are drills for skills.

A caution on overdoing it: Too many repetitions can be unhelpful. If you get bored or tired, you can lose focus and get sloppy in your movements. You are not developing the skills you want, and may even be ingraining bad habits.

Performance Practice: In performance practice, you include the full scope of your putting process, from reading the putt to reflecting on the outcome and learning from it. Performance practice should simulate real playing situations as much as possible. Use just one ball, and toss it onto the green as if it had landed there after an approach shot. Mark your ball and go through your full process as if you were on the course—reading the green, choosing your line, judging the speed, and executing the stroke. Be sure to include your post-putt routine, in which you learn from the results for continuous improvement.

Putting contests with a friend can simulate the competition and scoring that happens in actual performance situations. Sharpen up your routine by approaching these contests as if you were competing in a match on the course.

To simulate real playing situations when you're practicing alone, score your practice. Using one ball, attempt eighteen putts of various lengths: six putts under ten feet, six putts from ten to twenty feet, and six putts from twenty to forty feet. Record the total length of the putts you holed. Count how many three-putts you had from outside twenty feet and how many one-putts from inside ten feet. Try to improve your scores each practice session. To keep your expectations realistic and not get frustrated, remember the statistics from the chapter "Get Real to Get Confidence."

Always keep track of the most important score of all: how many of those eighteen first putts you *made*, whether or not you holed them. A good goal for your practice session is to be able to say, "I *made* every putt."

PUTT WITH CONFIDENCE

When a reporter asked him about the slow greens on the course he was playing that week, Gary Player said, "I love putting on slow greens like these." The reporter reminded him that last week he had said the same thing about fast greens. Gary replied, "Fast or slow, I love putting on whatever greens I'm playing."

Putting with confidence is feeling like you can make every putt you look at. You can't wait to get the flatstick in your hand and, like Gary Player, you love putting no matter what.

You can putt with confidence by focusing on *making* your putt—whether or not you hole it. Believe that your putt has a chance of going in if you read it well and stroke it well. At the same time, be realistic about the odds of holing putts so you don't get discouraged if a good putt misses the hole. Care about how you get the putt started instead of worrying about how it will finish.

Cultivate your ability to read greens. Develop a routine for reading greens, starting with the overall lay of the land for the course. Look for the high and low points around the green, find the fall line through the hole, and examine the last few feet of the putt. Get a clear picture of the line you expect the putt to take and commit to that line.

Fine-tune your feel for speed. Train and trust your hand-eye coordination for an athletic response to the length and slope of each putt. Hold the putter softly and maintain consistent grip pressure and tempo; just vary the size of your stroke for the speed you intend.

Groove a dependable stroke with as few moving parts as

possible. Find the best setup for you, one that helps you aim accurately and hit the sweet spot consistently. Feel as though you're *sending* the ball on its way, rather than *hitting at* the ball. Start every putt as a straight putt, chase the ball down the line, and hold your finish.

You can putt with confidence if you have a complete and consistent routine. The ideal routine addresses all the elements of a putt, one by one. First you read the putt and decisively choose your line. Once you've set up to that line, you're done with direction and should focus only on getting a clear picture of the speed of the putt. Trust your hand-eye coordination and roll the ball into the picture.

Be ready for challenging putts. Practice the techniques for dealing with difficult putts. Keep your cool and you'll be able to handle putting under pressure.

You can putt with confidence by working to continuously improve. Use every putt as an opportunity to refine your ability to read and your feel for speed. If you know what to look for, you can learn from every putt you roll. No matter how well you putt, you can always get better.

My purpose in writing this book is to help you feel that you can truly putt with confidence—that you can *make* every putt. I hope that at the end of every round, you'll think, "I can't wait until I play tomorrow, because my putting gets better every day."

Bonus Chapter

One for the Yipper

FOR EMERGENCIES ONLY:
HOW TO CURE THE YIPS

The most famous obstacle to confidence in putting is the malady known as the yips. It is so feared among golfers that many don't even like to say or hear the word.

When a golfer flinches uncontrollably just before impact, that is the definition of the yips. The ball doesn't just slightly miss the hole. It is not uncommon for a golfer with the yips to hit a three-foot putt five feet past the cup and on the next hole leave a similar three-foot putt two feet short. The miss itself is bad enough, but the embarrassment of such a display can be mortifying.

The yips are notoriously hard to get rid of. They seem to be so much beyond the golfer's control that some theories regard them as a physical malady or a neurological disorder. They have caused golfers to give up hope and quit the game entirely. Golfers have resorted to extra-long putters and/or strange grips to keep their dominant hand from taking over and flinching. Part of what makes the yips so insidious is the fact that they are reinforced in a vicious cycle. The instinctive reaction to escape them only intensifies them.

The yips develop when you feel particularly bad and berate yourself for missing a short putt. It's an experience of emotional punishment, and human beings cringe or flinch when they anticipate punishment. So on subsequent putts, you flinch when the ball is about to miss the hole. You start flinching earlier and earlier in the putting process, until eventually you flinch as your putterhead hits the ball. It shoots off in a strange way, and a new fear is added. You're not just afraid of missing the putt; now you're afraid of flinching as well. That's the start of the yips.

And that's why the yips are so hard to overcome. The flinching itself becomes a painful embarrassment, a punishment. You anticipate flinching, and the yips become a self-fulfilling prophecy.

Another factor that makes the yips so deeply ingrained is the human tendency to use the hands, particularly the dominant hand, for tasks that require precise control.

If you have fear as you swing the putter, your dominant hand will tighten and take control. For a right-handed golfer, that means the right hand tightens on the grip as the putterhead is about to contact the ball. The more fear you have of making a poor stroke, the more your right hand will try to take over, as if it had a mind of its own.

Golfers can become so afraid of yipping a putt that they freeze over the putt at address, unable to take the putterhead back.

One part of the cure for the yips is to let go of control. That's the solution, but the fear of loss of control is what causes the yips. So golfers think that to overcome the yips they need to get even *more* control. Perhaps that's why they're so hard to overcome—what you do to try to fix them makes them worse.

It seems like no matter what you do or how you try to trick yourself into making a smooth stroke, you yip the putt when the moment of impact arrives. Because the pattern is a self-reinforcing one, and because the experience of the yips brings out strong emotional reactions, it takes patience and persistence to undo the habits that perpetuate the yips.

As you walk to the green, or even think about putting, your chest tightens as though there's a steel band around it. You have trouble seeing the break, and have no feel for speed whatsoever. As you stand over the putt, there's a sense of panic, a blank and numb quality of not having any idea how you can get the ball from where it's sitting, across the green, and into the hole.

Those who are stuck with the yips can feel frustrated and hopeless, but there is a way out. In case you were wondering, what's in this chapter is not just theory. It's from personal, practical experience. I've had the yips. That's how I know exactly how they feel. But I cured myself of them, and now I'm putting better than ever.

The steps for getting over the yips are best explained by describing a series of lessons with a golfer named Larry.

Larry had the yips. He could hit towering drives, crisp straight irons, and had a decent short game. On the practice green he had a smooth stroke and rolled the ball well. But when we reached the first green of our playing lesson, it was a totally different story. Larry had a putt of about eight feet. He went through the same routine I saw him use on the practice green, took a couple of practice strokes, and took his stance. And then it happened. His backswing stopped short after no more than two inches, and he followed that with a quick jab at the ball, which jumped to the right and sped twenty feet away.

On the second green he had a putt of about the same length. Again he went through his routine. Again he made a cut-off backswing. But this time the putter stopped abruptly as it hit the ball. The putt went halfway to the hole and wobbled to a stop.

Larry was mortified that he couldn't get a seemingly simple putt anywhere near the hole, and horrified that he seemed unable to control his own arms and hands. Over the course of several sessions, we discovered some key pieces to solving his yips puzzle.

He was very comfortable making full swings, and even had a good feel for partial swings with his wedges. But when putting he had a very different stance and grip. It wasn't comfortable, and he didn't trust his stroke. He had no feel for the swing size he needed to roll the ball a particular distance. He was extremely attached to score and very concerned about what others thought of him.

No trust, no feel, and a lot of worry kept him stuck with the yips.

Larry needed to feel more comfortable swinging a putter and more certain about how the swing translated into distance. He needed to have a meaningful routine and be more attuned to his process than worried about his results. Together we planned his improvement program.

First he practiced drills for feel on the putting green, which helped him to learn the swing sizes that would roll the ball different distances.

Then he worked on creating a real purpose for his practice strokes. Using rehearsal swings, he worked on matching them to the length of the putt he was facing. He practiced reproducing the same size swing at the ball that he made in his rehearsal swing.

He became more interested in how well he executed his process, and put more emotion into his success at *making* putts than into worrying about holing them.

He practiced giving himself a break and not beating himself up if he missed a putt.

Larry's assignment in our next playing lesson was to make

a practice stroke that was a rehearsal of the swing he'd need for the length of putt he faced. He was then to reproduce the size and tempo of his rehearsal swing as closely as he could. Success was based only on how good a job he did of repeating his rehearsal swing. It had nothing to do with how the putt ended up.

Larry was very focused on guessing the right swing size for each putt and doing his best to reproduce it. He was determined to do a good job of that. On the sixth hole he realized that he'd forgotten to be worried about flinching. He got better at matching swing size and distance, and he began to snuggle his putts up to the hole. He stood up to a twelve-foot putt on the last hole, made a couple of rehearsal swings until he felt the size and tempo were right, and took his stance. He then reproduced that stroke exactly, without a hint of a flinch, and had the biggest smile on his face when the ball poured straight into the middle of the cup.

During a round of golf, the tendencies that reinforce the yips are diminished when your concern shifts from results to process. The way out of the yips is to turn your focus from the outcome of the stroke to your preparation and action. Focus on maintaining a constant grip pressure on the club, especially with your dominant hand.

Making the putt, rather than holing the putt, needs to be your reference point for success. The best way out of the yips is to make your goal on every putt to do your best to reproduce the rehearsal putt you made next to the ball: the same size, the same rhythm and tempo, and the same swing path. You have to abandon concern about the outcome of the putt.

Since the starting point of the yips involves self-punishment, you need to undo the habit of berating yourself and feeling embarrassed about having the yips and putting poorly. Taking yourself too seriously feeds the yips; having a sense of humor helps lessen their severity. Paradoxically, the psychological key to overcoming the yips is to accept them, not to feel embarrassed by them or to try to get rid of them. It's challenging to take such an attitude, but doing so is the first step in turning the cycle of self-punishment and embarrassment into a cycle of ever increasing trust and self-confidence.

REFERENCES AND
RECOMMENDED READING

Armour, Tommy. *A Round of Golf with Tommy Armour*. New York: Simon & Schuster, 1959.

Benson, Herbert. *The Relaxation Response*. New York: William Morrow, 1975.

Burke, Jack. *The Natural Way to Better Golf.* New York: Hanover House, 1954.

Chödrön, Pema. *The Places that Scare You*. Boston: Shambhala, 2005.

Farnsworth, Craig. *See It & Sink It*. New York: HarperCollins, 1997.

Gallwey, W. Timothy, *The Inner Game of Golf.* New York: Random House, 1981.

Hahn, Thich Nhat. *You Are Here: Discovering the Magic of the Present Moment*. Boston: Shambhala, 2010.

Haultain, Arnold. *The Mystery of Golf.* Boston: Houghton Mifflin, 2000 (reprint of 1908 original).

Herrigel, Eugene. *Zen in the Art of Archery*. New York: Pantheon Books, 1953.

Jackson, Phil. *Sacred Hoops*. New York: Hyperion, 1995.

Jones, Bobby. *Golf Is My Game*. London: Chatto and Windus, 1962.

Jones, Robert Tyre (Bobby). *Bobby Jones on Golf*. New York: Doubleday, 1966.

Kabat-Zinn, Jon. *Wherever You Go, There You Are*. New York: Hyperion, 1994.

Leonard, George. *Mastery*. New York: Dutton Plume, 1992.

Morrison, Alex. *Better Golf Without Practice*. New York: Simon & Schuster, 1940.

Murphy, Michael. *Golf in the Kingdom*. New York: The Viking Press, 1972.

Nicklaus, Jack. *Golf My Way*. New York: Simon & Schuster, 1974.

Nicklaus, Jack. *Jack Nicklaus' Playing Lessons*. Trumbull: Golf Digest Books, 1981.

Parent, Joseph. *Golf: The Art of the Mental Game*. New York, Universe, 2009.

————. *Zen Golf: Mastering the Mental Game*. New York: Doubleday, 2002.

————. *Zen Putting: Mastering the Mental Game on the Greens*. New York: Gotham, 2007.

Pelz, Dave. *Dave Pelz's Putting Bible*. New York: Doubleday, 2000.

————. *Dave Pelz's Short Game Bible*. New York: Broadway, 1999.

Penick, Harvey. *The Wisdom of Harvey Penick* [collected writings]. New York: Simon & Schuster, 1997.

Pennington, Bill. *On Par: The Everyday Golfer's Survival Guide.* New York: Houghton Mifflin Harcourt, 2012.

Shoemaker, Fred. *Extraordinary Golf.* New York: G. P. Putnam's Sons, 1996.

———. *Extraordinary Putting.* New York: G. P. Putnam's Sons, 2006.

Simpson, W. G. *The Art of Golf.* Far Hills, NJ: United States Golf Association, 1982 (reprint of the 1887 original).

Stockton, Dave. *Unconscious Putting.* New York: Gotham, 2011.

Suzuki, Shunryu. *Zen Mind, Beginner's Mind.* New York: Weatherhill, 1970.

Tendzin, Ösel. *Buddha in the Palm of Your Hand.* Boston: Shambhala, 1982.

Tendzin, Ösel. *Space, Time and Energy.* Ojai: Satdharma, 2004.

Trungpa, Chögyam. *Great Eastern Sun.* Boston: Shambhala, 1999.

———. *Shambhala: The Sacred Path of the Warrior.* Boston: Shambhala, 1984.

Utley, Stan. *The Art of Putting.* New York: Gotham, 2006.

Wodehouse, P. G. *The Golf Omnibus.* New York: Wing Books, 1973.

Woods, Tiger. *How I Play Golf.* New York: Warner Books, 2001.

ABOUT THE AUTHOR

Dr. Joe Parent is a renowned PGA TOUR and LPGA Instructor/ Sports Psychologist and a sought-after keynote speaker and executive coach in Performance Psychology for business. He is the best-selling author of several books, including *Zen Putting* and *Zen Golf: Mastering the Mental Game*, which have sold over a quarter-million copies in nine different languages worldwide. Named by *Golf Digest* magazine as one of their "Top Mental Game Experts" in the world, Dr. Parent helped major champions Vijay Singh and Cristie Kerr to reach No. 1 in the World Golf Rankings. He has coached thousands of professional and amateur golfers of all levels and all ages, and he currently specializes in working with competitive juniors. He teaches at the Ojai Valley Inn & Spa in Ojai, California, and at The Los Angeles Country Club. He also offers lessons by telephone or video conferencing to students all over the world. For more information, online instruction, and long-distance lessons, visit his website at www.ZenGolf.com.

CONTACT INFORMATION—
GOLF INSTRUCTION

ZEN GOLF® LESSONS:
MASTERING THE MENTAL GAME®

Videos, Audios, and Books
Online Instructional Materials
Training Aids

Telephone Coaching Sessions
Skype (video-link) Coaching Sessions
Playing Lessons in Person

To learn more, please visit:

www.ZenGolf.com/shop.php
www.ZenGolf.com/instruction.php
Email: drjoe@zengolf.com
Telephone: 805.705.0770

CONTACT INFORMATION— PERFORMANCE PSYCHOLOGY

The secret to getting the most out of your
abilities is getting out of your own way.

–Dr. Joseph Parent

AT THE TOP OF YOUR GAME™: PERFORMANCE PSYCHOLOGY FOR BUSINESS

Keynote Speaking
Executive Coaching
VIP Golf Programs

To learn more, please visit:

www.ZenGolf.com/business.php
Email: drparent@zengolf.com
Telephone: 805.705.0770

NOTES